MARRIAGE 2001:

A Bruised Odyssey

MARRIAGE 2001:

A Bruised Odyssey

POEMS & WRITINGS

By J. W. YOUNG

unPublications
1968 S Coast Hwy Nm 303
Laguna Beach CA 92651
www.unpublications.com

First edition: January 2024 *ex libris*

Printed in the United States of America

The publisher is not responsible for websites (or their content) that are not owned by the publisher.

Cover design by © boraart via Canva.com

Publisher's Cataloging-in-Publication
(Provided by Cassidy Cataloguing Services, Inc.).

Names: Young, J. W., 1974- author.
Title: Marriage 2001 : a bruised odyssey / poems & writings by J. W. Young.

Description: First edition. | Laguna Beach CA : unPublications, [2024]

Identifiers: ISBN: 978-1-963166-00-2 (hardcover) | 978-1-963166-01-9 (softcover) | 978-1-963166-02-6 (ebook) | 978-1-963166-03-3 (audio book) | LCCN: 2023923543

Subjects: LCSH: Marriage--Poetry. | Marriage--Literary collections. | Power (Social sciences)--Poetry. | Power (Social sciences)--Literary collections. | Family--Poetry. | Family--Literary collections. | Family violence--Poetry. | Family violence--Literary collections. | Abused women--Poetry. | Abused women--Literary collections. | Censorship--Poetry. | Censorship--Literary collections. | Women authors, Black. | LCGFT: Poetry. | Essays. | BISAC: POETRY / General. | POETRY / American / General. | POETRY / American / African American & Black. | POETRY / Subjects & Themes / General. | POETRY / Subjects & Themes / Death, Grief, Loss. | POETRY / Subjects & Themes / Family. | POETRY / Women Authors. | LITERARY COLLECTIONS / General. | LITERARY COLLECTIONS / American / General. | LITERARY COLLECTIONS / American / African American & Black. | LITERARY COLLECTIONS / Diaries & Journals. | LITERARY COLLECTIONS / Subjects & Themes / General. | LITERARY COLLECTIONS / Women Authors. | FAMILY & RELATIONSHIPS / General. | FAMILY & RELATIONSHIPS / Abuse / General. | FAMILY & RELATIONSHIPS / Abuse / Domestic Partner Abuse.

Classification: LCC: PS3625.O96436 M37 2024 | DDC: 811/.6--dc23

ACKNOWLEDGEMENTS

I'D LIKE to thank the writers, artists, and creators whose truths and harmonies echoed in my mind and served as my personal source of strength in these dark times—
Dr. Angela Yvonne Davis, James Baldwin & Frederick Douglass—
and those, such as Lanegan, whose art was strictly forbidden.

—   j. w. young

DEDICATION

To
Hunter,
"the future view in the rear mirror"
Lesley, Taylor, Penny
family

Disclaimer:

if you see yourself in these pages, please seek professional help.
the poetry and writings contained in this book were penned
from the author's perspective on the star dates indicated.
this book contains survivors.

Contents

FOREWARD

The poetry and writings deal with the confines of marriage when defined and marred by subjugation, domestic abuse, and censorship in modern times. **At a young age,** I left my version of paradise and was sent to live in a polar opposite type of town. I began writing poetry in my young years to cope with racism, rape and being alone. In college, my best friend and I were broke most days and **left to fend for ourselves**. She encouraged me to express myself and stop hiding my pain. Soon, I was faced with **an asshole liar and a liar asshole.** I lost my car and place to live, and therefore, my ability to be productive and independent. I was no longer able to get to work and faced more difficulties trying to make 3 nickels last for 3 days.

Leaving the trauma and violence of my school years behind, I packed up to leave that hateful place. Heading out of town with a friend, I overheard a caller in the background, saying nigger 5 times in 5 sentences. Who still talked like that? *Everyone...everyone...* the friend answered. **This was a stark reminder** that I did not belong. I was very tired of hearing those words and the daggers that fell with them. **I admit,** it was tough on the road, but **nothing prepared me** for what was ahead. I endured an abusive and violent marriage for several decades. There was no choice but to cope, and I did so, by writing out of sight and under the cover of darkness for fear of backlash. **Anytime I was caught writing**, an argument would ensue. There was no time to edit nor revisit the works which were kept hidden. **Many of the original writings were destroyed**, so this book contains the survivors and represents a voice of endurance. Yet, no matter how difficult the journey was, God told me to write through any adversities. This book is an odyssey into the human condition. **Follow the journey** of hope, pain, grief and the difficult pathway to reclaiming a sense of self.

'90s

musings on torn pages

Once I touched the glow of truth. Passion. Before I settled

in, it was gone.

Rebuilding a life after bury of snow. Regaining the

strength and the care.

- - - - -

the hope that I care for.

- - -

Do I have to keep it?

the pain they have caused

I've not known any other way since.

Now the attacks won't go away with the passing days.

I used to wield my pen to reinvigorate.

I use it now to shield his offenses.

I used to adore our relationship

our love relationship.

- - - - -

what motivates your brutality is the fact that I don't

black: sheets, windows, walls, threats
i don't leave the room
don't know anyone
the music blares all day
basements.

I hope to get that credit card soon.
still dealing with it.
panic attacks worse.
I can't go in stores.

**I've got two jobs and
homeless
pregnant
frozen milk
eggs from the trunk
puking into empty tuna cans.**

Homeless. Hotel. Homeless. House. Move.
homeless.

You Leave Undone
5/7/98

If I was over there right now, <u>she'd</u> be fixing my food
otherwise known as
You do a lot of things for me, but there are a lot of things you leave
undone.

Today I look around the room of my child, I begin.
I began pondering a path towards a goal, my own.
Today, as yesterday, I am surrounded by this beast and his burden.
I began preparation for this today, degraded by love enabled by fury.
I begin my days with a thrill for the new, that end with chills when you
enter my view.

What has become of the me and the you?
Who two were created.
So, I'm here to serve you?
I'm here to gift to *you* the future?

Where am I?
Trapped in a lie.
"You are prey,"
It eats me alive in this present.

Today I write but hidden from view
to re-discover my better path.
Of course, there is nothing
to this pen defiance
but your wrath.

Love given in pleasure.
Love returned dead in threats.

"You do know you must moan?"

Whatever it takes,
Create yourself another fake—
Send yourself to the outer zone.

For the Master

1.6.2000

Every day I am sent to get clothes for the Master. Today I awoke, chores were undone. Folded but unhung clothes were still stacked at my feet. Upon hearing the daily rude directions, "go get my clothes! get me dressed—Now!" I arose and obliged by pulling a pair of pants out of the stack. Going for the shirt, the Master yells,

"What the fuck! Don't be so damn lazy!"

Lazy? I pondered. It was me getting clothes for him because HE was too lazy and spoiled to do it for himself! Oh, but of course, that matters <u>not</u> to the Master.

"I'm in a hurry!" The same old line I always hear.

Obviously frustrated from my earlier refusal of his Romeo proposal, now he gritted each word he uttered with every hurried statement. He picks up the phone and calls his Mistress. Mistress, the phone goddess. I feign enchantment. He takes 17 minutes this day to ease his consciousness and reset his gentlemanly demeanor in order to claim ignorance of the voice of spousal dissension and bellows,

"Who me? You upset?"

I enter the front chamber to revisit more unfinished chores as he continues to amuse the phone Mistress. Now off, he resumes to clench his face and pumps his fists in anger.

"Hurry! I need to leave."

So, in an effort to not fight, I give my son some clothes to offer. And as tradition runs, he refuses my new selection, opting instead for the clothes at the foot of the bed that I "lazily" gave him the first time. Today's game has run.

Now he will enter the world's crisp, cold, darkness and bask in the company of his silent enemies—the doublespeak, backstabbing, dominion of friendships & business contacts—or so they call him to his face. This is where we enter the *Whatever...* zone.

> "Oh...I am in a <u>good</u> mood now."
> "Well, you already made me mad..."
> "Oh, ..." (slave girl)
> "...Finish getting me dressed!"
> "...Do my hair!
> "...HURRY!"
> "...Find my hat!"
> "...Screw off!"

He yells. And yells.
Every second, hope is carefully diminished by the tone he sets.
Eagerly awaiting & assisting the Master's departure,
I dream of a day of difference.
Yesterday, I read my astrological prediction
that announced my marked determination and need for survival,
that I must climb atop the doubt wave and ride success goals,
that my intention in each quarter will be bold and benchmarked by the outcome.
No.
Who am I?
I am the slave-girl.

1/18/00

For the Love of My Son. Change.

Today. Today is Thurs, Jan 18th. I have much to be thankful for—bouncing and bounding in a half-size body. My son brings me great joy…to meld and mold his creativity, his personality. And, he keeps my view on life quite positive.

However, one thing I've never synthesized completely has been my relationship with my spouse—I give this to myself. For my jewels of compassion are raped and displayed for the admiring masses to enjoy. What deception, a mere mirror of happier times, this has become.

What happens to a woman struggling to support those around her? Those whose main support escapes and is gifted to others in cultivation. I can calculate the odds of gain but they will be most weighted against those of distrust and distaste.

For in another time, I had relished the thought of perfection. I kept my distance from both internal and external dramatic absorptions. However, I am displeased with my relationship. It has withered in respect and association. In the past, I released all of my bonds to create a single strong one. However, that is being regurgitated and thrown to me in the form of courtships and cultivated enemies.

I could do without that struggle that comes with the disrespect.

Disrespect <u>is</u> becoming so common in my life that I find myself in this new dawn attempting to carve out my prior self from the mold of another's creation. I have distanced myself from an aching need to participate emotionally, to bridge a chasm to the new age. The touch of another outside this realm has been burned and the desire has grown latent. The passions I hold are no longer waves of movement to change, but furor in which arguments and mistrust develop. I have not allowed myself personal joy in my new capacity. The streams of consciousness I normally would delve into have fallen into the newness of an armored existence.

To what do I owe this existence—not life—but existence?

My beliefs and tolerances are abusing my structure & growth. The pride I once felt as a partner has diminished into modern slavery. *Only a mouthpiece for what I've been given*, is how I am seen. My native magic is curtailed yet given away freely in efforts of cultivation of new prodigy—when it is my foresight that allows me great distances. I have allowed and practiced this new form of slavery daily. It is no less mentally painful in this day than my forefathers' plight in theirs.

Today, I will continue in great change.

'00s

musings on torn pages

From the mirror I went.

The smile reached across my chin;

eager, anxious for new times and new memories to fill the

pained places.

From head-on, I would witness the risk.

Playing chicken with metal sculptures.

Word warriors trying to get the cut, the opening, the past,

the portal.

Not willing or relinquishing.

From this, I join the future.

The child smiling in the backseat that I see and laughing

in the mirror.

No veering due to fury.

Keep focused, the road's reappearing.

Focus on the future view in the rear mirror.

- - - - - -

Wandering through the flames

the burns singe the syringe

Death prepared behind you.

Fan them and they will smolder the hopes of family left

standing.

Avoid them and we live.

Enjoy them and you die.

Period.

When the Mother's Dew Freezes

When the mothers dew freezes, and you partake of its blindness, where do you leave yourself when you're gone? While you're gone? With each step into your hidden dimension you arrive at a new dementia.

Do you soak up Hate's seed to plant it? Does it ever leave from you other than your mouth from which to sprout? Yes, it is angry at the loss of your soul. Your life, direction and intention have met goal's intersection. Sorry is covered with it. Who loses? You're embodied with gifts from the ages. But, demons are wretched in those abandoned places just watching you slowly let go and solemnly walk away. They don't realize that you have many truths to misplace and a chasm to fill between time and space.

When you do regain memory, you wrestle between the two.
Night walks, you're a living corpse.
Day shines, it's a glimmer in your eyes to bring you back alive.
Astray, you're embracing blindness.
Beasts on the beat appear to feed freely on your carcass.

Invisible grips keep you restricted while moving.

Who must watch you within your pain?
Me too, he too, are we to watch?

That pain you'd never admit that you're in because the sniffs and lifts are genuine?
Dealing a hand to the gambler, you continue to indulge unaffected.
Excuses become goals.

> "I don't mind, I don't need it." and,
> "I don't need it, right?"

My own doubts appear true.
I know you hate me so why don't I leave you?
Who's to say when you will return from this well—
poisoned, or cleansed or as roadkill.

1/18/01

What a motherfucker could & should know about his wife

Always trying to run past shit.
Think that dicks run the world and always tryin' to get in 'em.
What's up with the lit when you're afraid of the pen?
I know. You running scared.
Put on the lines about hoes and bitches.
You're just wishin' that was your situation so you might have something
for bitchin' about.
And did I say *bitch* about you?
And your swinging dick.
That don't make you a real man
only a shell.

Oh, pack you a bowl?
Trim you a line?

If that's all you care about,
bitch, go to hell!

Can't handle the re*a*l-a*c*tion-ships I have with other men.
Trick! Fuck you with all that other jealous shit.
How 'bout you grow up and join me in the lead, not in the end.

When will you learn to be glad with the gift,
instead of missing the feeling of running your lip?
Next time you want to sess', go grab some weights,
or, shut the fuck up and pack your *bitch* suitcase.

You call me Dolemite when I talk back

Like you're the only rhymer in this family pack.
You
wish
bitch!

I have the power to run things without that dick.

Fuck off.
Fuck you.
Fuck this.

Always trying to judge me by the dollar these days
while I'm skating thin ice and nursing you back to life,
you ain't <u>had</u> to work since we landed on these shores.

What were you thinking when we were apart?
Skanking like you got no heart and no partner left in this relationship?

But that don't matter
it's like a thing of the past
now bully-you want to cover your ass?

Wanna work with me just to keep me down?
Ding, ding, time's up.
Get the fuck out. Get the fuck on.

1/20/01

Time to start the "Ho-Bitch List".

Introducing, an icon in his own right.
Tonight, gallantly brooding with the dumb-bitch twins.

> "This historical day", he proclaims,
> "this day, my $10 whore to my right (uppercuts with knowing
> right eyebrow)
> and my $5 boy."
> "I've made the finest purchase of all."
> "I seek re-election!"

"Such a pompous ass!" I laugh to myself. When they are reeling in the
ranks beside me, I'll recall it was so brazenly made with ass breath.

> "If you don't have anything good to say to me, I get a refund."

Be happy for the time the Goddess has blessed upon us all.
Riotous acts of indecency abound.

Now that I've been molested by uttered discharges of bowel filth foul,
spat shrapnel of hate and anger,
now with "the world done 'em wrong" look
that is so easily stretched across his blank disgusting face,
now here come the shriveled hands of no-man.

Shriveled to bits of no good, where good was once so keenly implied.
Now they move too brisk for any discussion.

Each mongrel can take its place at the base of my cold heart and
piss.
That place being as fluid as my own bile.
That which I entrust my followers to gladly take.
Bile atop my decency
and yes, piss for it needs to pass.

Even with determined yet lethargic palm
the thrust of my pen to paper offers less of a challenge.
Even with the most pristine of innocent pleas
unchallenged vultures continue their sweep above to covet their prey
beneath.

Vultures.

"You, my mongrel, worship me…" the prick thinks to himself…
itself.
"What riotous wench doth have her cavernous ways about me,
and can eat me?"

The mongrel thinks, oh, no joy.

"Nuzzle me and my slight imperfections too. Do please, give me
a break."

Prick, put your head down.
No one wants to hear from you.

[It retorts with]
The Ho-Bitch List of Do's and Don'ts
1. Don't smile.

2. Take it, like they take it from you.
3. Fuck "them" & and they know who they are.
4. Enjoy.
5. Take it back & put it where the sun don't shine (yes, that'd be the heart)
6. Digest.

In the story of the ten dollar and the five dollar, here we come to a crux.

Ssshh, now let the mongrel speak.

"Ah-hum,"
but like clockwork that cuckoo calls it.
Ssshh, now let the ass-fucker speak.
Or, maybe let's let the TV talk.
No, let the prick speak

"The girls all coo, why not you?"
"No shit."

it declares to me.

1/20/2001
Torture

The torture of our sisters
at the hands of man.

Can we move to unearth the distorted tree roots
to be removed and not multiplied?
Our essence mass exiled to an isle of serenity?

We can gather and scatter in the swollen night,
each personality a cornerstone of freedom.
Goddesses of nature and nurture indeed.

Where these daily permissions, called marital rights,
thefts of innocence, mishandling of body will never begin.

Violated, violated, violated,
violated, violated, violated.

Such is this, fear's negativity has ensued
and now marks my soul.

I'm not worth your time?
Just a tease indeed?

Frustration yields madness when your bloodhound barks at my nature's
driving force
and is the greatest collapse to the sanctity of women's course.

Magic yields madness when pent with vulture pets.

If only they were just pets.

And...

(Interrupted)

(Continued)

I was just asked if I were going to be barking all morning.

After I've been barked at all morning.

Swell.

And...their ignorance was bliss.

musings on torn pages

Hope, up,
    Music, down.
        Life, up,
            Growth, down.
    Moving up,
        Family broke,
            Family broke down.

Born into a slavery of modern-day,

Now forced to expand my craft and to officiate impended freedoms

for myself and own my son's sake.

1/31/01

Elevated

Out of the beast of burden a new day is dawning.
I've left the son-of-a-bitch and it feels great.
However, I do give in.
It's shameful to have him assume.
His current fuck is an enemy,
of mine and his future other.
Oh, the tall tales I could tell.
Of *his* house, *his* money, *his* this and that other.
My mistakes have dug my grave even deeper and deeper.
I've sheltered our lives with intangibles—work, love, support....
Not to mention food, rent, house, and cars full with gas.
I've found a new life, a new light, and a new path.
I want to spend my remaining days here in this city
with my metaphysical lovers.
They hear me.
I call their name but have always refused pursuit.
I know with whom I want to share my energy truth
and who values it.
Today I will toss the line.
I do not ever have to give to this one,
my sensible old friend.
They only ask to do for me.
I will follow
where the love I need is
blessed be.
For the mornings haze has cleared
& my heart remains broken
but it is mendable.

And today, I begin.
I feel again.
Pure energy in
thought and prayer.

2/2/01

Today is the second day of the second month of this millennial year.

I am humored at the approaching and passing dawn of the day here.

Last eve, I delighted myself to care and learn in the capacity of strangers.

Today, I bask in the knowledge that my spirit and my craft are becoming re-engaged.

It is with great honor that I've achieved this lease on life.

I recognize and remember passion, to be captured and rapt in its fleeting moments of borrowed time.

Rituals of day and night magic are shared on auto by my mind and soul.

They blend to breathe life into this battered and beaten body,

I am

lifeless to emotion from previous days but renewed and invigorated with this new life's charm.

I am

a geode forming from toxic waters dried by mother's fire and held up by father time's arm.

It seems like mind clouds keep shifting from vapor to liquid to solidify matters, but tears have outgrown this.

And, they are still leaking.

Finally scorched away, I regain the ability to see the beauty in life and even people.

I recognize my gladness for partaking in nature's celestial thrust when speaking of life.

2/3/01

Ruts,
stuck without luck.
Found,
in stones that jut down
to the floors of cavernous valleys.
It was my intention
to react in an abusive manner
but highly unlikely, as
that love is enamored.
There are schools of thought
that are created from a massive passing.
The true priorities of thoughts unveil the eyes greatly.
There is nothing left to this scripture.
Once it ends
only fear forces a new one to be written.

2/3/01

Too many articles of frustration.
You must enjoy
or it will be withdrawn
like sleepy grass when touched.

2/6/01

Waves, Tides and Turbulence

42

If at every corner of the world you face rejection
the elasticity of feeling and emotion
are re-shaped to create a portrait of self-loathe
and self-hate.
Once the sky returns from burning,
red gives rise again to white and blue
it stays hazed by doubt
finding a hidden
(unfinished)

2/8/01

So how do you know when it's over…an enthralling delve into the limits of tolerance and *(unfinished)*

2/13/01
Part I Declaration

Today was a day of declaration and release. My husband declared the following:

1. About giving up his mistress—"what no more sex?"

2. (He) has "to be honest, it will probably happen again"—translation, I will not give up my side piece for you.

3. "You can have sex with men"—you are free from this marriage. I cannot give up my side piece for you. We are no longer bonded.

4. "I am only doing what she wants me to do"—I have accepted her as my controller.

5. "I'm helping her with her sex issues"—I am tired of helping you with yours.

6. "She's going to make money for me"—Just like you do, so why stay committed to you?

7. "I can only take so much"—There is a limit to our love, even marriage.

8. "She gives me what I need"—You do not.

What does this mean?

He has made his choice, and if I cannot accept it, then we are finished.

Goodbye Doc Tryin', my man, he no longer exists.

2/13/01
Part II Nothing in your eyes

45

Over the years, I've been reduced down to nothing in your eyes.

On the verge of oblivion, I know that the true you & me do not know each other; even with all of my pleas for help.

Trying to work together, to stay together. The face you likely see is made up of tenses—of which it is difficult to discover or discern which is the orator.

But when I look into your eyes, I only see a little of what was, because your spirit is being moved by darkness itself.

I am a seer and your life's breath has been removed.

Your eyes are gray with hallowed soul de-fused.

The you that I see does not want me.

My love for you lies still and cold in armored awareness.

What I am dealing with now, however, will seal our fate.

3/29/01

Grasping

Encapsulated and confined by the sheer blast of positive energy.

A combination of pleasures and excitement.

But, within the walls of uncertainty lies the true quotient of base fear.

It is a base fear brought on by negativity.

The best indication of a perceptive change is the recognition of human magnetics.

Pre-preparation is obvious and central to our fruitful existence.

We can all stand from a positive head change.

I'm energized by the possibilities of sunshine and rainbow spectrums gained from curiosity.

3/30/01

Out of Reach

Today, my creative vision is blurred.

I've endured yesterday and was sent forward into today.

I'm tired physically and spiritually,

I'm moved.

Endurance breeds strength and longevity for mental creativity but it is all
a test.

I've entered into new territory,

new chasms have been crossed and depths uncovered.

May-June 2001
Silent Frustrations

From day one it was a partnership of support. My beliefs have allowed my naivete to flourish, in love. In the beginning, there was an offer (*Master censored*). An offer of platonic love and trust in order to reach a golden dream of success. Now there is frustration and sadness in realizing love's full potential.

"Where are we now?" I ask. Broke, poor, and rich only with principle. Principle too is questioned, as hypocrisy engulfs action and exists by persistent inactivity. What has been moved besides our positioning in the universe? So what's the story?

At Odds

I've never met such an immature man besides, oh brother. But, ah there is a king! Arising each day with cartoon animation to drown out the genius thoughts that cause him great grief...

oh that would be hypocrisy #1 -- TV.

Animation not to be interrupted by casual or business conversation, because you know, that would be rude. In some intellectual conversations, it is lauded as the downfall of the American community.

It is proclaimed by others to be the leech that transfers the blood of a nation into the marketed and pre-programmed human machines born of both government and corporation. But it is, in fact, a soothing four-sided orb full of reason and relaxing entertainment (huh?). Basically, it most often only serves as a tool for bickering amongst the humans in the home.

The brain of the king relays only outside interruption from someone other than an immediate family member. To be engaged? Don't bother (Chan is only a 30 minute show you know). Oops, now I've stumbled into hypocrisy #2 - Family vs Acquaintances. If your last name is not the same, you have propelled yourself to the top of the priority list on what words penetrate his perception.

Love

…After 27 years I still question my capacity to understand love. Not in the sense of giving or receiving, but embodying the precious gifts of love.

I spent 7 years knowing love as an emotion that drives and directs my very existence. Now, after betrayal, I know the essence of unconditional love. Never before this seventh year had I ever questioned my depth of commitment so intensely. I've come to know that great divide between everlasting love of children and a committed love to a spouse.

Now reality has swept its vicious venom-tipped dagger into my life. I feel the difference between the two, where there once was no question nor divide. I'm drawn to tears when I see my child's face glow while basking in the newness and innocence of youth. But now I'm drawn to doubt my own capacity to restore the unconditional love I held. It will return, I believe, but my love has aged into maturity carefully and precisely molded from hurt.

Recognition of Death

Upon recognition of death, comes change.

Love Affair with Love

There are times when I do become engulfed in fits of passion, fits frothing rage. When do you come to terms with the swings from nightmares and the hollow darkness of this feeling?

remnant

I have a life that I expected to lead: we all do.

Now, torn to bits,

hatred in fiery words.

Spewed anger.

I have a goal.

And, I have a reason.

The goal is life.

The reason is seven.

"What did you say?!"

My tone got higher at that point. There's so much to be said in silence. And, this range of insight suddenly drew in a close-up. So much of this is old, so old that it is still new. A shitty different day. Stinks like yesterday's waft. The sunlight's broken shine into my cracked bedroom window warned me of another day ending in glass shards and bloodstains.

"Here we go again!"
He stopped and stared and contorted and conjured. What his face expressed. What his lips let slip. *Once again*, I thought, but refused to speak.

"What did you say?"
Now I'm watching him shine in the dim light of the living room—anger glowing. He pursed his lips and his teeth laid bare. He chokes a cough like he needs to spit and gurgles,

> "I said, I would be with my elbow to your mouth and knocking your teeth out!"

Hmmmmnnn, I thought.
"For being honest!" I shouted.

I blurted out in disbelief of how many years I've been fighting back those words. Those words cornered me in this room. But those words became a clear, clear shock to all the violence and all this brawn.

I shrugged, just bored of this shit. Think I'm going to S.O.S.? Too bored to react. Too bored to cry or to hover, to cower, or stammer, or care. So, I turned away.

"You're going to elbow me in the mouth for being honest!"

I must have had my hands on my waist. I felt my own strength deepen the squeeze to my hips—posturing. I'm angry, now burying my fist into my sides.

"Whatever!" I tossed back in his direction.

The nonchalance of their presence in his ears were just a taunt to him. I didn't care. He didn't turn around. I have returned, solemn and unashamed for finally telling him the truth. Before there was a wall there. I think I moved a mountain.

I saw myself getting used to this. Cracking nervous laughs and trying to hold up my head for another day. Another grim day in and another cruel day out. I'm fed up with this shit. At this point, and without needing to take another stand, I just retreated. I escaped to the bedroom and got undressed. Finally, I felt like I had my own skin. I felt my dignity. I finally exhaled. My stand was met with the boiling blood.

"It that a threat?!" he says.
"Is that a challenge?" he begs.

How do I respond? I ask myself. And then, there's the names he spews,

"Cunt!"

Vapid off his tongue. I guess that's what weak snakes say before they strike. But, no. He proceeded to tell me how I was affecting my own karma.

Oh! For the years I've spent holding my tongue and now letting it go? For getting thrown to the ground? Being choked like a dog on the floor? When gasping but unable to fight back? When at that point between death and life?

I wanted to know, but I already saw my son there. His eyes sparked a beam of desperation in reflection as his daddy tried to strangle me on the floor. I saw that sparkle he had, a smile he beamed, before worry widened it. I rolled hard and away from him. Rolled as fast as I could on that laminate floor. The laminate patches darkened from his daddy's danger lurking above me.

I am. Being silenced by a pair of hands squeezing tightly. On this floor. In this house. Struggling in front of the sofa. Muffled. Yelling for help between gasps of the air. Grabbing at what I could while falling.

I'm failing to stay alive. I tumbled somehow and it was over. My son staring into my eyes. His eyes tilted to my level. The same level low. But no, not today. I can't get into this. I cannot be your punching bag today just because I was honest.

But I was.

> *Earlier when riding home from work, I gazed at the waters dance. A few animals were greeting me, it seemed they were really grieving me. Some were still, guiding my path.*

I ran to the mirror to look inside myself. Beyond the broken neck and fractured exterior. To find the me not controlled by violence. The me not getting gripped and ripped with fear.

Knowledge is power, angels chanting at me on the way home. I gripped the handles of my bicycle tightly and reflected. The rush of heat swarmed me and the gash on my dome cinched. At 105° F today. I stopped at a park. I don't want to go on. I decided to take my own pace.

Me, let's not be so easily controlled. We were never promised eternity. But losing time is guaranteed. Why let anyone take all of you? You were put here for a reason, right? Life already showed you about abuse. Wasn't your youth an introduction? I felt the spirit of my grandmother console me.

Time seemed to move backward in this day but I returned home. I've been left to fend for myself, you would not even drive me to the bus stop. Because, then he whines, he'd be "obligated to pick me up". That's pitiful, I thought. That is wrong. But I couldn't care less today. I knew what was coming. Never able or willing or conscious enough to help me. No, not me. It was three years ago that he was fucking the hippie bitch. Asking me to take her home; sweaty and heaving from fucking all night. Bullshit bitch. Couldn't even speak. And why didn't I drive that car into a ditch? I don't know. Play nice. I'm thinking to myself. Play nice. Why? He's not begging me to death. He's worried about this naked bitch and her ass that gripped tight in his hands—fucked her on our bed. So I took the bitch home that night and on the other nights. He wanted to make sure this bitch got home and didn't have to spend all night waiting for the bus. You mean…like I do every day and every night—writing, waiting? Running to the stop before dawn. Pitch black a.m. outside at 5:30. The hours to ride home exclamation point…but hey, that's me right?

(U C, he's walking away now. Not listening. Don't care, couldn't give a damn. He's leaving now, gone...)

I couldn't get anything. I got threats. Just for finally telling the truth. Now telling me again about his client.

"Oh yeah? You thank ME…"
SMACK…an exclamation to his point.
I'd only see the back of his neck bulge as his body was heaving away from me.

Now. No smirk, no anger, no smile. To play it safe, I'm folding my clothes. Putting away my things. Putting away my fears. Putting away my life. I look away. He's still there. The room grew. It recoiled to a spiral downward as the shock settled in.

I've lost my fear of violence. It is the regular occurrence. I've given away that childish fire I had. And the one quick to rebel. It's boiling anger now. I looked at him again. The door closed some, but not all the way of course. He had to listen in, had to check, if I was moving.

Did I survive his attention?
domination?

"Bitch!"

He quipped, while still holding the door that his fat fingers gripped. Four fat inches from the top of the frame. He stood braced there hoping for a reason

—to hit me some more.

"Come closer."

His grip on the door widened. I kept still. He stood glaring there searching for a reason

—to hit me some more.

I've seen this before. Bored. I've seen this, you just want me to surrender! So you could come on in and hit me in my face? Or on the head? Or maybe the next leg? Or, capture me and wrestle me to the ground? |*CHARGE!*|

—to hit me some more.

So I fall to the ground. Hoping that the next one would be the last. What more? I'm bored of this.

"I just want to spend time with you."

Been awful to meet you heavy Dom Greasy, begging you Dom Greasy, begging you now for my life?! No, not anymore!

Today, I said, "Thanks, dismissed!!!"

And his brow stiffened. He lifts himself off me. I could have said anything but nothing.
Instead of nothing, I said nothing more.
No fear, no pain, and no care.
No threat. No more.

"What hurts worse than hate?"

He would always tell me this…he would always ask me, bringing me closer to him by popping the collar ring on my shirt.

"What hurts worse than hate?" he barked and pulled me even closer in today.
"Indifference" he growled and spit stuck to his lips.
I think to myself, "you're right and I am."

PART II.

|SCREECH|

"What did you say?!"

The bus driver pulled up to the stop and opened her door to me.

"What did you say?"

She nodded to me. I moved in closer to see her smile display.
"I said to bring on your smile with you," she said.
I froze up. She closed the door and nearly drove away.

A smoky steam mix covered me.
I almost fell down where I stood.
The sun was static scorching overhead.

I looked up for a quick assessment as to the basis of my motivation for living another day in scorching sorrow. But, before she left, she smiled once more. I turned to follow her orders. I wasted no time bringing my bike aboard on this particular day.

I had pedaled just slow enough to keep from drenching in sweat on my bike ride to the next stop up the road. It was 12:59 p.m. I'd missed the bus by 10 minutes.

But, earlier this morning, I'd left in this same hurry to escape his company. He was watching TV then, smug about not taking me to the bus stop today.

"You got a bike!"
He yelled, yelled and yelled.
"You got a bike! Do-it-yourself!"

Piss poor excuses. "Of course you won't take me," I muttered, then left. Sleep is the only thing you want to do. I heard him rambling on. His words had trailed at my back.

While running out then, I had met a woman in the hall. She smiled at me too. I tried to use my hoodie to cover my swollen face.

Returning to focus now, forgetting about his words haunting me. The bus driver with smiles steadied the bus gently in the road. I walked my bike off the curb and hoisted it on to the front rack. I climbed aboard and we shrugged knowingly about the bruises I was hiding, once again.

"Look, they're only with their women because they're horribly afraid of being alone," she said, "That's why they don't leave…you've got to leave them!"

She grabbed her command wheel tighter and heaved her chest forward, huffing as though she had given that last bit of advice to some other damaged bride too many times before. I tried to interject, but she went on, not at all interrupted by my attempted responses.

"There are a few good ones…If you raise 'em yourself! Hah! Or you have to steal 'em!"

The bus driver's route eventually went back around. She rounded the vessel to the corner I knew.

"Next please," I quietly told her with a nervous laugh of course to follow. "Uh, I suppose there are those that do good things?" Shit! I sounded hopeless. Hopefully hopeless. "I'm not bothered if someone did something for me or not…uh, I…"

Her eyes grew in the oversized rearview mirror. "What's his name, love?" She poised the steel vessel forward with eyes still reflecting me.

I didn't answer. Didn't have any love named for me. The man I married was gone. Just, the shell, the big baby abuser. But, words didn't escape me.

"Well honey," the gentle-worded driver shrugged, "we don't all win the lottery."

"You go on now and do your best to stay safe tonight," she tossed, then turned her smile away while approaching my familiar street.

"Next stop, please."

I couldn't wait to get off the bus. I knew I didn't have any smile left today. But, I knew I really needed one. What did it matter, he'll just knock that smile right off anyway! What does it matter?

"Next stop, please."

PART III.

Back home later that night I pull open the screen and unlock the main door.

"Why do you have to be such a cunt?"

There was no other greeting.

"Well, you can answer me!"

"Who, me?" I responded.

"Why do you have to be such a cunt?"

He's carefully putting on his shirt. Reaching into one arm hole, squeezing it above his non-muscles and inserting his head to be threaded where I can wish I would morph and attach a noose.
He is glaring at me.

"I'm just being honest." I walked away.

Obviously, he was shaken. He started to stammer. I couldn't believe that those words finally came out of my mouth. It's true, I don't always want to have it out with him. That doesn't mean that I'm being dishonest. I'm being very honest about the way I feel.

He braces himself in the doorway, clasps his arms one within each other. He is searching, hoping to do something—anything, that allows him a chance to knock me down to the ground and choke me again.
More taunts come.
Then bullying.

He's been going to new classes lately.
Learning to manipulate my mere presence, my reach, my grip.

To silence me.

No strikes. Not for this truth.
Why don't you wait for a lie and strike?
Why do you wait to deny that my truth makes sense?
Something within you is sick.
Be a member of humanity.
Your illness is what you're using against me.

But, at least for now, you know
the "truth" is I don't want you anymore.

June 4, 2001
When Will the Pain Subside?

My head begins to throb. My own warm blood pulses through my veins. Frustration clouds my vision in the pouring rain. How do you recover from betrayal? Each day I force myself to believe I can achieve that balance but my heart is still hollow. The golden keys to love's eternity are still dangling from love's strangulation. I've been bitten in the past, but not by an equal.

Today my outlook changed and the instability I've tried to repair is again the source of my grief.
I must confess to myself that I do have needs.
I have to confess to the world that my needs are important to me.

Once, I remembered that I indeed walked this path alone but I am forced into submission
based on class and sexism perpetuated by my own partner.

Never did I see this growth take shape.
Misdirected energy and focus.
All the losses from deception and rape.
My soul is writing this in angst.
And in hopes of blossoming from death to rebirth.
I must be mistaken, I tell myself, but my heart is certain.
It is broken, bent, pained, and hidden.

It has finally refused to be chided into healing for the sake of fighting off confrontation.
I want to retreat for a while and take my mind off of suicide's goals.
My thoughts have not traveled that road since high school graduation.

June 4, 2001
When Will the Pain Subside? (A Companion Poem)

Love. My head begins to throb.

His shadow of shame hovers and darkens my vision.

A heavy dose of his love beats down on me with its frustration.

He unrolls his sleeves and like a burdened boulder heaves himself forward.

Hefty beads of sweat cascade off his brow, stinging his eyes and covering his coward.

He squints and strikes; landing just short of his target.

That's all I can see before the impacts repeat.

My crown cracks, blood splatters, a socket's blown out.

I'm bloody. Irrelevant.

Fear grips but broken teeth don't chatter.

Crimson spit torrents, barreling down over my enflamed lips for a potent mix.

Bloody mouth gurgling, drowns out my pleas, once clear now changing.

Drops litter the ground, my shattered gaze follows them down.

How do you recover from betrayal?

Like a fool, I think this bout's over.

But my mind is relenting, I can't think straight while I'm staggering and struggling.

Pummeled. I'm a heap of thoughts and emotions.

Lifeless on the ground, waiting for rage's act to be concluded.

Where did it get me? Bold strikes sear from the edge of nowhere.

Encircled in a chokehold. Wound in love's stranglehold. Getting love's boot end.

Vows sealed, forced to submit, now I'm told, "Woman, mind your place!"

"And, if you ever leave me, you will die!" was my wedding night promise.

Then I spoke up, was derided, but laid a death blow to your ego.

So now you say it's me that's out of line and all wrong.

Wrong color, wrong class, wrong sex, and wrong race that brought this on.

Wrong temperature of your coffee and its splashed in my face.

Never had I imagined this would take shape in my mate.

Instead of love, you focus fired energy into strikes and blows "for love's sake".

I must be mistaken, but my heart doesn't tug for this kind of damaged love.

It is bent, pained, and broken.

It's pleading my needs for you to set my neck free.

It's fighting off the ragged emotions my cracked dome brings.

It's begging to stave off confrontation when my pride is already lower than my knees.

> "You can say what you want, bitch, but I won't hear it; I gua-ran-tee!!!!"

And, here, he comes again towards the target and that target of brutal love is me.

June 5, 2001
The Shelter

After 18 calls and 3 hours wait, the office phone startled me awake. It was after 1 a.m. when I had escaped and fled to downtown on this bitter cold night. The phone rang shrill into my ear beyond the shock and tears. I received word back from a crisis counselor that a shelter bed had just been vacated in a neighboring state, but they'd have to put me on a waiting list for it. Hope collapsed with me in my seat.

One hour past that frustration, a better call rang through. She said that I would get a room. I had silently fled to the safety of the office tower where I worked. I repeated the words with my retreat as I left my office in a sick kind of hurry to get the last bed.

"Four o'clock a.m.", she'd said. I was too early, so I drove around to kill time. After a while, I pulled over and parked in a lonely alley. I got out and cinched my hoodie straps. I didn't have any extra clothes. I looked into the misty surrounds and saw the meeting point. Here I was but nothing else.

I stood waiting at the meeting point weeping with the weekend rain in the darkness. I realized there was no phone at this meeting point and got frustrated. "How do I reach the shelter?" My lifeless body propelled to walk. I went back to the car. Driving around, I just kept searching. I finally found a phone at a nearby gas station and dialed the number collect.

Away from home, battered, and alone, I looked forward to a warm bed and a night's sleep. My last coin slicked into the slot and I pressed on. "Hello?" I heard right away, glad the person picked up.

When I arrived, I was buzzed in and so began my ascent into the building of the hollow women's shelter. Three sets of sunken eyes met me with half smiles that night. Although their bruises shined in the dim lights, their smiles were appreciated.

All throughout orientation at the shelter, I looked door-to-door for the crying room, but there was none. I couldn't imagine what we were supposed to do to cope with the problems that forced us here, when our body mechanisms require endurance of emotional pain that is released naturally through tears. There really was no place where we could shed the layers of hurt and come to grips with our new beginnings.

Struggling for composure, I was oriented into what would be my home for a while. I took this change in stride as most of the women here had been here before and their understanding gave me some space. Assigned my chores and shown to my room, there I saw my roommate, Jeannie.

I had entered the room on the first night too timid to awaken her. After this first night there would be no other normal nights indeed.

Jeannie was in her late fifties, still clinging onto teddy bears and warm fuzzy slippers to bring her joy in a storm of vengeance. By her own admission of truth, she had again survived a severe physical and emotional beating from her estranged husband and landed back in the shelter.

She spoke calmly but uncomfortably to me. What I learned about Jeannie was that she worked full-time but she had, nor has, any ambition. She talked of few hopes, but one that was critical was moving. She spoke to the walls often about her troubles in order to cope. I don't get the sense that Jeannie's mind would even pair up the pains from these recurring violent experiences with her stays at the shelters that she's been in.

Jeannie was struggling to get enough money to travel to see her family. At least, that's what she said. Later, I found out that it was her mental instability that would cloud her dreams of escape. No spirit in a bottle could even help this Jeannie, left broken and close to death.

Every night, Jeannie's dreams of violence echoed in moans beyond the midnight moon's glow into our barred windows. She awoke very rarely, but I, often. I could hear the pain in the bellow of her moans and groans…of "no, please, no" and "you can't stop me, no..." Her voice always trailing off as she would bury her face deeper into the pillow. I would hear the rips as she clawed away at her pillow while ranting at her dream foe. She put up a hell of a fight every night. I was sure she'd like to forget the fact that her dreams were just replaying her horrid realities.

She rarely ever slept without a light next to her bed and it always beamed down into my eyes. Her bunk was next to the door, so she would prop it open with a chair and let the hallway light halo her bed. Already tossing wildly from her dreams of torture, she awoke me again each night, slapping the walls while searching for the light switch. The lights comforted her, they made her less afraid of the dark that brought on the sleep that brought out the demons of her violent dreams.

Yet, I let her get away with it. I'd rather hear her sleeping soundly and cover my eyes to the light, than hear the wails and cries she let out in fear brought on by the darkness. At least I could cover my ears and eyes. She could not recover from her own mind.

For the next few days, I stayed in my assigned bed. I got up only to call in sick to work. The team at the office was totally supportive. The Director there ordered an advance on my paycheck so I could afford to buy food.

Finally feeling like my eyes could see straight, I felt it was time to move beyond my bunk and the phone. I got dressed and huddled toward the kitchen. There were ladies in the hall there with two and three little kids— ranging from one year to about ten years old. Some were running around; others were just sitting quiet on the bench.

I finished up and managed to get down to the kitchen without anyone stopping me. We were allotted three shelves of food in the kitchen. I looked for the shelves marked with my name and found nothing but a can of beans that I could eat. Everything else was pasta, cheese or some other thing that I was allergic to.

Back in my room, I grabbed my stack of clothes for the shower. Both showers were closed now, so I took a wash-up in the sink in the bathroom. I thought about my son back at the house with my husband. I imagined he was there with me and smiled into the mirror. I loved that child more than myself and I missed him like crazy. To talk to him on the phone would require that I talk to my husband. That wasn't something I was looking forward to just yet.

We only had a few rules at the shelter and we could leave temporarily. I escaped out into the day and immediately felt like crying. I held back the tears as I ordered a hamburger at a diner across the road. I grabbed my order so fast that I almost left my drink on the counter. Struggling to make it out of there without eye contact was work.

musings on torn pages

How do I regain my strength? You're pushing me, and it's just eerie theory.

--

I regain my thoughts with numbness. It's all a possibility.

7/14/01

Excited at the allowance of freedom.

I'm struggling to produce a new face of happiness without my son.

I know that I'll return to grace and restore the unit of family he knows.

7/14/01

The escape is as lucid as the dream. The dreams I carry have been marked with choosing a new path. I'm grossly uninspired. I try and determine the loves long lost and their impact on my most impenetrable visions. I cannot forsake my life for the longevity of Hate's breed.

Violence is simple when it is not paired with love.

A partner offers a place surely filling for the heart and soul. An attacker offers a piece of the reality of death and condemnation. When a partner attacks, there's no way to redraw the lines—the boundaries of life or love. It becomes a quest for survival when trust is pushed to oblivion by violence.

I don't know any worthy attackers. Particularly when the memories formed are my own. I used to rebirth my path for a love relationship. But with my neck almost broken, my breath cut off, and kicking and screaming like a dog on the floor, today's sunlight offers me another chance awakening for change.

I begin the day on this journey alone—me and my credit cards, trying to get across the country to rebuild myself. Yet, there's nothing more catching than a vision of my future. I have many delectables to offer another man (or woman) —healing, teaching, spiritual exploration and excellence. Hours of imbalance play a true role in the inception of what is allowed to be right or wrong in the world. But my newest memories are of writhing around on the floor, fighting for my life.

And now for the escape. Do I need to love another to be whole? I'm starting to recall that it isn't what makes me whole. It only sets me on a new track, then forging my path back to what is truly me. Now battling with a rip in my core, I find I am still not healing from these wounds.

Battling, as it may be, I will not underestimate the determination required for achieving a balance.
Never have I been set on such a crucial path for renewed existence.

Now I am unafraid.
Fear is no longer my biggest enemy.

What I seek for myself can be better explained by stark revelations in honesty or sacrificed in death. I make no mistakes in tackling fear and wrestling it to the ground. There have been many trials and tests of patience. I plan to travel, regain my strength and fury. The travels will allow me to ingrain my thoughts with newness and possibility. Integrating my ideals and my emotions can be a test of the highest sort. I cannot relate the disgust I feel for the losses that are soon to come.

There will be all types of crossings that will come before me. I cannot determine which I will choose to explore or enjoy. I persist to indulge in any experience of further journey in this state.

Taoic and tantric are the rhythms of the future I am trying to reel in closer to me. The best defense of parallel emotions has to be an intrinsic selection of difference and a manifestation of existence.

July 17, 2001

I Think I've Fallen in Love. Again.

…Deep in the voided chasms of their eyes
the blood vessels chart the path through to their heart
I want to reach inside the caverns of their chest
to massage the love expired back from death.
So we can both heal the wounds inflicted by deception and lies.

Do I love the eyes?
They're like mine.
The black-rimmed pools
brimming from fear and abuse.

I return to behold the armor you've built—as have I—and we are both shrouded in it. We share many tortuous experiences that keep us connected to the past.

But for now, I do love as strongly as I can. In my mind, we live in independence and in unison. I close my eyes and see you blow me soft wishes that are disguised as air kisses. So often I want to hold you and show you true eternal transcendence. I am glad that we don't need stolen kisses to warm our reality in this dimension. Time is for our own good, we must personify and grow patience.

Tonight when you sleep in frustration, in the bed of deception, dream of my return. Or come nearer by allowing your heart flight with mine to intertwine. I do love you, sweetness, our days of black death are no longer. Live the few moments we are given by showing your inner core and truth's light. The love of the day lifts us both higher to fly into the clouds of harmony, and at night, bathing in red wine. Join me in every dream and make it tangible when I return.

The love I hold for my spouse is so lost in servitude. The pain is removed with each breath while thinking about a future with you. Our blood is thick to sustain. Our desire as friends is just currently hidden. This may exist for a short time in order to renew. It offers our past a chance at being forgiven too. Don't hesitate to love, to live…please don't deny.

Will we pay for this sacrifice? Of course,
there's always a test in that cross we must bear.
Mine will be pain, and yours in sorrow, but do not get jaded in the losses.
The ending, that is our beginning.
I've seen you from ages before dear friend.
And you the same have seen me.
Don't forget the evidence that comes from higher empowerment,
the spirit that swells the trees.

From the grips of the reaper
those we part from will be shown what in life is truly fair.

Join me as a love in my life, as a friend and a guide.
Stay to remind me, as a friend, that I don't have to hide.

I love my spouse but his grip on me only grows more evil and tighter.

I cannot undo what he has done to me but I will not fear finding love for some other.
I could not cheat, as some do, but my mind will not be regulated.
Love born as friends between us will be true and not fucking sedated.
It's time that my freedom weathers the grasp of my own hands & to cut the apron strings away.

July 19, 2001
What Love is This?

How can I carry on through life without truth? I'll never pass through the gates of the elders holding on to love for another. Through many dimensions we have traveled. How can I give in to the temptation now?

At best, I bemoan the days of the past,
those filled with uncertainty and scarred by violence.
I lift my head up higher now and over the clouds
to reel in the stars and revel in the density of their silence.
But I must return back to my bed, one made for me and by my own self,
to lie in the lies of passionless hell.

Too soon I will return to my husband's grip.
Back to normal for he, but not for me.
I'll be left muted and empty.
I imagine those same days playing that same old song.
Love being lost and wondering when he'll slip.
Betrayal since past but did he ever seek my forgiveness?

"Not wanting to rehash this," he said, so damn adamant.

I refrained and withheld my kisses.

Am I true to the sages of my native lore?
How can I be content if my mind is running to lust like a chore?

Let me through the gates of consciousness.
My longing is not lust.

But love for another?
No advancement without provocation
and that will have to sustain us.

Questions are few, I know what I want.
I want to be free from violence, control, rape, and submission.
I was once a respected teacher, now I am being told to go back to school.
I cannot implore much commitment when in total disregard of convention.
A unity of equals is not our foundation.
I have been put on a pedestal only to be stepped on in advance of <u>his</u> higher station.
That's not true love that can sustain the ages of eternity.
That ache is only a means, a vehicle, of dishonesty.
As you creep through each night hunting for prey,
I have to live as your wife, smiling the hurt away.

I think of old crones nodding through time—
hiding for revealing to their husbands that they do love.
I recall old men, held up in creativity's respected light,
still clamoring in bathhouses,
a blow out of mind, out of sight.
I think of those whores dancing before blue and green lights,
shaking it hard for the Owner's red-hot club night.
Girls of the evening swirl to take home enough pay
before their husbands return from overseas to see them again;
these ladies of the evening, women, whose jobs jade them from love's desolate reality.
Whores, you might say, do not qualify for love that can be kindled.
But for me, my mind runs rampant in the thought of touch from another.
I revel in the joys that could be possible with a new love.

From afar, I watch, a fantasy that seems so simple.
To look, but not touch.

In my mind I give freely, my affections purely primal.
I've created an affair with love that will never be easy.
A whore of emotions that cascade upon the broken sworn shores of marriage and commitment.
My thoughts untrue, but my actions as the good wife, remain consistent.
To continue to serve the man I did marry, but my mind is at sea, tied up in fantasy.
I know my body resides in this space in time,
but yearns for the closeness of some other mother's son.
Some other one.

All of these thoughts remind me of love that's gone,
those who have to hide their desires to become one with another.

For years they must hide behind the farce they cannot escape.
Is that my future? Will that be the rope that keeps me with my mate?
Where do those souls go when death deems them free?

They must come back and try?

I see through their eyes, this hidden rage covered by lies I cannot profess,
and truths I must deny.
I hope there are not years associated with this diminished wish.
How horrid life is when your destiny is without true love's bliss.

Enjoy the desires that are stirred.
Face facts that love's within reach and must be bold.
I am married by choice from the start.

I now see the pit of longings that I must avoid

in order to remain at bay from the true feelings of my heart.

In reality, I vault that love away.

But, endure as I must, fate deems that it must fade.

I know that now these feelings never die even when the water turns to

clay.

July 19, 2001
Trying Again (A Companion Poem)

This is the third time I've left.
Is it my destiny to return?
Will I again be sacrificed at the hands of fate
forced upon due to rejection?

I'm calculating my own demise.
Deep in your throws of violence.

I've found the threats and calls for destruction
do not eat at me anymore through sleep nor wake.

What's left of this existence?

Vivid and lifeless, I remain involved in my own destiny.
I will start a new chapter bound by love's eternal light.
I'll hide my passions deep in my mind.

Mask on.

8/16/2001 to
8/17/2001

Today I landed on my neck.

Pushed off the bed onto three glasses of water,

a water pipe, and a bowl of caramel cups.

This time I landed on my neck.

I saw that face again.

Madness, hatred, and disgust all twisted to instill terror.

It glared at me for one split second

before all the colors in the spectrum blanked as I tumbled backwards off
the bed

opening my eyes and struggling to get off my neck.

The thrill is gone.

August 17, 2001
Waning: Property Rights

I envisioned providing natural touch, healing energy, limitless love and the offer of a tribe as my gifts to bestow upon my mate. And I did. Now, our lives are filled with battles. And in giving, I have become an element of property.

For years, in sickness, I provided—only to find that you believe I own nothing—not even the rights of my body, mind or child. If you make a quick recollection of thought, I have been a "good" wife in the sense that I have not come home from sleeping around, wrought with disease; nor have I chosen another mistress over you; nor have I betrayed you by beating you in acts of dominance; nor have you been kicked and screaming, writhing on the floor under my grip—forcing your last breath and final memory to be that of me in control of you; nor have I sought the services of a street whore to satisfy me in your absence; nor have I caused you terror in what was to be the safety of my arms, only to be pushed blindly backwards onto piles of twisted glass.

If only I could reverse time—that's what they all say.
All the food, gifts, clothes, and bills I paid as you lay,
now weeping and suddenly unable to groom yourself?

If I could only reverse time.

Now I am a thief?

All the magic I've taught you, you attempt to use against me.
You've told me to go back to school because you can't appreciate my healing.

I'm told where to put my healing hands, and who's allowed them.

But, what you continue to ignore is that hand that feeds can be bitten, as
you should know each time you raise a limb to me in anger.
And a bitten hand can also retract.
How many more days do I have to fear for my life?
I returned to you yet again because you *needed* me.
Now you tell me to go and claim to be sick of me?

I don't want a partner that betrays
and to have to wonder when those flashes will come one last time.

I don't want to be referred to as a bitch, or listen as you tell my child how
stupid I am.
I don't want to hear you tell my child, "tell your momma to shove this up
her ass" and watch him bumbling back to me unsure just what to say.

I don't want a partner who finds it okay to delineate every facet of life
against me.
Every day, I hear "what's this shit about?" and "what the fuck is your
problem?"

You are teaching my child to disrespect women
by your daily acts of disrespect.

I don't see it ending.
I regret everything I've ever laid down in my life to offer you.
I am run over with your disrespect.

You communicate with me by cursing me and expect help because you
"need" it.

You have become an animal of inducements and a monster of one big inflated ego.

Seek peace, it is a necessity. I was not your enemy.

P.S. You have many kind words for strangers and loving strokes for whores whose game is rewarded. I believe it is time for us to find a new path. Where is it?

Sincerely,
Your wife, not your property.

9/14/01

No, I'm not cool with that. This is only one day of many.

My time in this gone town has been filled with separation, degradation and humiliation.

A chronology of jacked experiences.

cars, cars, no friends, no names

Panic. Panic. Panic. Rooms. Rooms. Rooms.

Panic. Panic. Panic. Rooms. Rooms. Rooms.

Sleeping under ice sheets.

Frozen hands protect the truth. And, you say to share the blankets.

Why must I give all to you? Because I'm a woman?

When we escaped leaving racism and hate, did I matter?

When sleeping in the car homeless at the mount in the dead of winter, did I matter?

For months, while working two jobs, pregnant and living at the rest stop?

While digging in the trunk for dinner?

While thawing the frozen eggs on the sun soaked hood?

While hoisting a hot plate like Flo to serve you between my work shifts?

Or, when my son's bedroom window was shot out?

We were lucky he slept with us that night.

Or, when my car windows were shot out? That fucker sped off threatening to kill us after I fed him dinner.

Now, no one wants to rent to us.

They just make that twisted face when we show up.

Won't even let us fill out an application.

Foreword to Slum 1.

Can't afford the bus token.

Walking in a foot of snow with no proper coat.

"Good enough for now," I'd say as I stomped and sloshed 3 miles to work.

And, that salad lady screaming at the black dude.

He'd handed her money she wouldn't take.

Fuck, that's wrong and I'm sick of it.

Store guards always following me to my car. Yeah, fuck them too!

Bobble bitch screaming at me for petitioning outside the store.

"*Bitch!*" Don't tell me that shit, lady! Had the nerve to spew her brain pus
at me.

"Bitch, I'm dealing with it!" Finding every job possible, so I can keep my
dignity.

Bitch!" I hauled off and hauled ass,

until someone killed my next car.

I'm walking and working.

Then someone plowed my van. I'm walking again.

Then someone killed my…fuck! Yeah, let's stop, it's car-less again.

I'm past past-tense with you.

You laughed watching me heave that giant laundry bag onto a skateboard
to go the Mat.

I started to hate the sound of the overloaded wheels drag after a while.

I hated every part of that parade.

Loading it on my back to get it out the door, heaving it down the stairs
and loading it onto a never ridden, prized skateboard.

Fuck, I hated that and this.

And, he won't help me. Ever.

> *I'm busy, that's your job.*
> *I'm tired, that's your job.*

Marriage is not my **j-o-b.**

Only a prelude to Slum 2.

Trash behind the fake wall. And randos, randos, randos!

I just prayed, I just prayed he wouldn't remember it!

Wouldn't have needed it at all because I saved the $ made from throwing
newsies on the lawn at predawn since we couldn't get any other jobs.

I made a promise to never be homeless again. Get it!

Instead, I'm stuck with a different deal.

Mold lined the tub from end to end.

A flopped house. Bugs eating bugs.

We'll make do, I said to myself. But, make do for what?

What are we doing?!? Another basement.

Shower works if you stand in the mud. And no walls.

Water seeped to join my grief every time it rained and formed puddles.

'Three months only' had suddenly grown longer.

Waiting to bathe…bathing at work…trying to look and be normal.

My patience rotted. The vermin lurking got stronger.

Unknowns coming by all the time asking for things.

Do you live here? Can I get an answer?

People never leave when the pots are boiling.

Nine bags of trash behind a wall. We're supposed to live here? This is why the bugs have beards.

I'm hoarse from cursing at the landlord because I was threatened if I didn't.

I'm told to play my role and thank them. I'm told to play my role and thank them.

I'm told to play my role and thank them. I'm told to play my role and thank them.

If I had a real you here we wouldn't have to be in need.

I'm looking for a time machine. I can't make it appear.

We fled haters and racists to habit like this? I hate that place!

And, this place too with you, but I can't leave.

"Feed the masses, girl, feed the people." Beats beat, beats beat.

I'm hidden to avoid the steeple piercing and randos are fucking in my son's bed.

The only people that can hold a conversation about reality these days are the ones that crack pills and inebriate first, lose self, or the perverse caught by chance out in daylight.

Only one stop was left before destruction.

That last shroud of decency pierced by a pin pusher with little care for my cause.

Then, months of failure. Years of opposition.

Now, here come these new ones.

They've started this new trend.

They all dress just like him.

They all say nigger this and nigger that.

Like it's okay and it's NOT!

You want me to carry your farce to new depths of ignorance?

Get yourself a clue.

Rap to your mirror and ask to borrow some sense.

Rap to it about your new liar's face.

Rap about being top dick and getting all the pussy you can chase.

So smug about your this and your that.

Disgusting as it is, it doesn't hide your fears.

Only 30 days you'll last and fate will pierce you awake.

What goes up comes down with a vengeance.

Check yourself in that magic mirror.

Taste the last of the pseudo life that you've modeled after mine.

Can't get it right? Kiss the crook of harmony and delight.

They'll make a terrific carbon if you're starving.

Stop cursing the person that sheltered you through each dark night.

Appearance

01

Riding a bus. Thinking of a movie about thieves & sex.

Missed my stop because I didn't realize I was really on a bus.

Looked out the window. Dark gloomy night.

Realized I missed my stop for real, so I rang the bell fast for the next one.

Creepy. Dark branches swaying.

Walked across the street. Went to the middle of the yard.

There's my boy. Sitting on a couch under the flowing tree shelter.

He was picking at the little lime buds on the limp branch above. A rag dog lay at his feet.

"What are you doing out here?"

I grabbed at him. I forgot to say hello.

"Papa dropped me off here. Said he'd be back soon."

He forgot to say hello.

I sat down next to him. His eyes chased the darkness around my shoulders.

I saw a cell phone in his tiny hands. Looked like a detonator.

I saw four wild looking dudes coming down the sidewalk carrying beer cans coming towards us.

One jumped over the side fence.

"Switch!" I pushed my boy and he rolled into the cushion.

I reached across and braced my arms to protect him.

"*Wassup!*" I yelled.

We stayed still.

"Can we come in and *stayyy*?"

Damn rando tried to act nice and talk to me. I felt a little scared with four dudes acting out but a mom can't show that when they're protecting their son. I look at over and my kid's bowed up with fists ready. He raps my waist and looks up into my eyes. My boy wasn't scared so neither was I. He's way too little to <u>not</u> be scared.

Time *to get out of this whole situation, right now.*

"You just jumped the fence, fool, you are in! No way, get out of my yard!"

They kept on egging until I scrambled call that spouse.

"Where the fuck are you!"

"Why?"

"Where the FUCK are <u>you</u>?!"

I get black.
Luckily, the neighbor guy wearing a dress rolled by on his bike.
These jerks find something else to do.
The punk in the yard backs off and runs while I'm still yelling.

"Asshole! You left our boy out here at night by himself? You crazy?!?"

"Be home soon." Click.

Too real.

Across the street, I saw a neighbor's light on.
Music drifted from another home.
We crossed over and I started dancing under their carport.
The more I danced, the more the problems felt smaller and shorter.

Then, my boy took off running.
        "Just wait, momma!" he said.

"Where you going? Hold up!"

His birthday shoes lit up my life in the night.
I chased him down for a bit.
He stopped and we fell together,
laughing in another neighbor's lawn.

"Okay, okay, Mr. Sprint."
We stared up and grinned at the sky.

"Now, let's me tell you a story about the fairy guy I met…"
I finally had him to myself.
I hadn't seen him for quite a while.

"The fairy I met, was as small as a bird, fluttering against the screen of
your window."

"As small as a bird, momma?"
He stretched his arms up like wings.
I wiggled his hoodie back down over his cheeks and went on.

"Yeah, as small as a moth even. And he looked like you with a wizards'
cap and gown,"

I trailed off and on, and in & out.

Seven turned to midnight.
He's fast asleep in my arms.
The rain danced to my cheeks and I arched to cover his.
A song played in my head as the cars going by played their hiss.

Seven a.m. gave in.
We're still waiting.

9/19/2001

How much shit can you stick in it?
What's the point to say refrain?
You don't feel our pain.
It's been years now since.

How much shit can you stick in it?
Said it's no longer about me.
Trying to make things work but you're outliving life in front of the DVD.
Our little boy's growing without being told but his mind perceives.
Each dawn I wait for things to stack up. I struggle to be free from misery.

How much shit *can* it take,
that untamed and bloated frame?
I followed where your blood and spirit flowed,
now we're all misdirected,
now we all run shallow.
can't hide this anymore.

October 8, 2001

I See You Again

You came into my life again, I dreamt.
"How do I keep love away? We're bonded."

Shaken and scared, I unveiled my fears.
I'm close with few, perpetually a short distance from tears.

I see you again, this day,
Earth tilted to a new axis,
a new and unmapped lunar route,
where I am not a matrimonial captive.

October 8, 2001
Wishing Days

…Firmly in your grip and well within your reach.
I listened carefully for your heart's tones.
I heard the swelling ocean currents beat the beach.
I listened to every word you made real for me that morning.
I heard you finally speak your love, recorded in Akashic memory.

Come closer to me, make this promise endure.
Your drenched words must repair thousands of shards to make this glass heart cure.
De-ice it from the bounds that have kept it fractured but pure.

What was said, I passed on, like a book of tall tales.
Compelled to share the essence of what was once only in prayers.

That day has come and gone, Springing forward and Fallen back to unwind.
But it is remembered well and the words of love remind.

October 17, 2001
Days Like Today

Then there's days like this.
You give me reason to grieve.

Moments shattered,
rewritten prose by candlelight,
my stashed and rehashed paper disorder.

Poetry unearthed now in crumbled type,
bits falling around me like the spit of a volcanic uproar,
paced panic thundering towards a fast overboil inside.

If I utter another word,
all vocabulary will be immediately tangled in the cords of my throat,
so I close that door, since you remain unmoved, by bitter pleas of
"no, please, no!"

Dearly, I wait.

I crouch down considering the peril of disgust,
but recognize the familiar fist,
ready to be restored to my face.

Gashes in walls and fragments of plaster,
blasted to confetti when my body impacts it.
My mind is chasing eternity through hallowed consciousness halls.

Caverns run deep with icicle thorns,
my mind is torn like this falling poetry debris,

you're unconscious to our value and inner workings.

I'm heading down with them to join the earth's sunken horrors,
to transition my position into a melded mind ore,
and remain stoned with the sweet vowels of tonight's sacrificed word
hoard.

musings on torn pages

10/17/01 I tire easily believing hope

Breathing the fresh dew, its scent upon dead roses, scattered in forgiveness of fate.

--

01

4th to LAST

Turn the day pale

Allow yourself to receive peace

Expand your vision to scale

Elasticize your memory

to include the joyous, unanimous burgeoning of life.

Bend through the burdens of times own truth.

Bear the weight of dawn's sorrows.

Join in the state of tomorrows.

Tell the tales to trinity for the sake of your own power's sake.

Generate an eloquence to call out spiritual warfare.

Remember the substance of use and abuse.

Harness your power.

In all dreams we have a future,

to be called forward

and return back to our body as Warriors.

It's tough, but really the same now that I know the drill.

Parts of man, parts of mass,

we'll escape without losing our ass,

once the old council parts ways

to save us beyond these few last days.

01

3rd to LAST

Crusted with your breath of vision.

Loss enamors your face.

Cum stains watermark your cheeks.

Depressions shatter your soul.

You reek of hope shattered.

Spilling over your chin like drool from your last meal.

Haunted by chains of submission and paralyzed by the truths of

(unfinished)

01

2nd to LAST

There is a way to address the needs of common misconceptions.
In the article "The Crises of H.S. Let Them Eat Cake," *(Readers...he's here)*

01

LAST and FINAL

Assholes—Assholes—Assholes…(censured by the Master)

How many people go through life without seeing the tunnel of filth from the inside out?

You crawl, you slide, you fall, you slide, you breath, you slide,

you talking that shit and stringing that thread.

A thread of truth that ties these lies together.

You band together the vibe & vitality of strength.

Can I help the fabulous?

The beginning with me starts with a beg. (censured by the Master)

a Kiss!!!

~~BEG~~

Peg Leg

Med Fleg

Bleg Pleg

As Long as it Rhymes!

(signed by Master censurer)

'02

musings on torn pages

Felt like I was on the game show. My turn, in front of a ticking prize clock, in front of a crowded audience.

"Hi, my name is ATM."
"Hi, my name is ATM."

allowing for no effort this time, and

June 23, 2002
An Idiot

I must have married an idiot. One who believes that battling a point to ensure that there is none is much more critical than widening the field of truth to reach understanding or merely acceptance of difference. Luckily, I will write this and he will brazenly state that he doesn't understand it and mask with innocence 'it doesn't make sense to anyone'. Poor boy. Tough luck. Your dinner's ready!

There are others who want to understand me.

June 23, 2002
Dear Wife

Here are the rules. Now that you've been beaten, and have returned, everything you say is a lie.

You are negative about each and every facet of our life. You say that you are joking, but I hear the hate. You say that you're waiting for me to call like I said I would, but I never said I would. That is why I am going to humiliate you today and every day from here on out. When you speak, I am going to railroad you into a lie. When you try and tell me your vision, I am going to make out the details as false duplicity and force you to fall over your own words. When you say that you love me, I will tell you that you don't. When I say I'm on my way, I won't be. When you think I am working, I'll be playing. When my playing is over, I will not come home. When you reach over for me, I'll push you away. When you smile, I'll call you evil.

Now you are alone. You work from home—with no friends nor relatives that will listen. I am going to keep you from the night. I am going to incite fights from my distrust and impose my rule against your happiness. When you think I will let you out of my sight outside of the house, I am going to follow you. I don't care if it's to the bar or to a priest. When you leave, you will take my cell phone and call me at every new place you stop. I will ask whomever you are with to validate your story. While you sleep at night, I will be checking the caller ID. I'm gonna keep you in check.

When you argue with me, I will ask you to repeat your problems so I can repeat them back as lies. When you tell me you're worried, I will force you to skip over the parts where I may play a role and point my finger at you. When I do let you go out…which I never will, but I will keep telling you that you can so that you have false hope—see, it's fun to see you get so excited! When I do let you go out, you have to find your own babysitter.

I have you and you cannot escape. When you want to break out, you will stay home and I am the one that's going to leave. You think you're winning, but I'm the only one playing the game.

When you feel like I am cheating, I am going to act as though it is your madness. I will point my finger at you and remind you that you don't really know me and the way I operate. When you want to talk about getting back on some kind of track, I will change the subject and make you take the blame. When you want to know when I'll be home, I'll tell you 'whenever I want to be'. And, you know I don't hear you when you yell.

Don't you know that I have friends listen in on our phone conversations so that I will never be a villain in their eyes? And, I will never be the villain in our lives. Don't you realize that my friends are going to come to my side when you try to intimidate me into telling the truth for a change? Don't lose sight of my duplicity. When did you believe I would drop my maleficent attitude? It fits! I have friends now, so I don't need you, and they will never see it or see you. They validate my honesty and they support my truth that you call lies. Who's going to give you protection from me now? Who is going to want you and why would they? I own you!

When we talk, now you know, my friends will be listening so that you cannot defend. You'll never be able to show your face in public again. I don't want to be anywhere near you, but I will ask you to join me so that I don't feel like we are at odds. When you say I am shady, I am going to ask my friends what they think. When I'm out alone and you want to talk—well, I am going to be living, so you better keep on calling me and expecting nothing. Better yet, don't call me at all. I have other girls that give me the things I need.

When you pay the rent, so what? When I pay the rent, you are living off of me and not supporting my ways. When you pay the bills, so what? When I pay the bills, it better be breakfast in bed and all my fuck needs better be met. What a better way to stay strong than by controlling you?

I am going to degrade you. I am going to reverse any words you say and all details that you bring up as a problem. You must never bother me. You don't dictate to me. You want to know my schedule? You are not worthy of reply.

What makes you think I want to be a part of some ritual of love?
What makes you think that you are worthy of an honest apology?

When things go wrong for me, it is because of you. When I don't make my money, I am going to call you and tell you to stop hindering my progress. When my friends don't call me, then I will keep you up all night to tell you to stop your wickedness. Why I don't want you, it's because you make me sick. When I am mad about you taking away my pussy, I'll get it on the side and tell you to be jealous. When those girls don't want any more of me, I will tell you it's your fault. When you tell me they are not worthy, I will tell you you're a bitch. When I have enemies, I will make you confront them. When others use me, I won't stand up, you will call them and complain.

Don't tell me where things are around the house…I don't want to know, that's your job. Don't think you will receive even one hello when I come home. When I am ready for you, I will let you know. When I don't want your cooking, you will pay the finest chefs to feed me. When you ask me for new clothes, I will tell you you're fat and you will buy me a new suit, hat and matching shoes every month.

Whatever you want, don't ask. When you want to go to back to school or get a degree to get ahead, forget it. It will always be me first because there's no you.

I'm tired from telling you the rules. But just so you know, it is no longer me and you against the world. No, it's us—me and my new homeboys—against you.

I'm busy. Go make my food.

And P.S.
You better never do anything like this to me!

June 23, 2002
Tree of Destruction

How I ended up with such destructive frustration, I wonder.

She once chased me into my room with a broom. She threatened to burn the house down around me because I was evil. She said I wore too much black, that I didn't talk anymore, and that I came home from school then immediately closed myself into my bedroom every night.

He was a workhorse and absent. I learned how to run my life like work. If I'm not working, I'm not being productive, then I fail. I always fall hardest when I'm not working. If I'm not working hard enough, with my hands in five or six pots at a time, I've already failed. I come down on myself with enough damnation for ten men. He said I gave up too soon, that I didn't have confidence, and that I will one day succeed if I would just focus on myself for a change.

The former was too distracted. He took my innocence and destroyed my self-worth. He tried to teach me lessons on behaving like a woman and left me to peddle my emotions like a whore. I sought out men for closeness, but looked to no one as my savior. I became sick and buried the fetus in the dirt. My mind carries the tomb in my heart. I immersed myself in work to overcome the denial. He said I didn't act like a girl, that I was useless if I wouldn't be with him anymore. Said I didn't support his habits well.

This one says he's sick. I gave my love and then became his nurse. I supported him through school, music, sickness and in life. Yet, he tore at my body and ripped away my dignity. He sits on the phone with a friend for backup. He cannot handle confrontation and suddenly needs the company of other men to make him one. He says I wear too much black, that I don't look like a girl, don't satisfy him in bed, can't make up my mind, am psychotic, and I work too hard.

My son always sees me sad. He asks what he can do. He says I work too much, that I'm more mean than nice, and asks why I don't love his papa anymore.

What do I think, what do I care? I care too much. I am a workhorse, work is my life, black is me—inside and out—and all of these things will be the death of me.

To my son I say love, to the others, goodbye.

June 25, 2002
Dead Air

I answered the phone when it did not ring. The operator told me there was no time for my call. I wondered if the operator knew that I was close and there was 'only time' for my call. The operator said that suicide garners no friends. I told the operator that the suicide was within them. The operator took my message and told me they'd call back when the line was free. I called back an hour later and the same operator took my call. The operator told me that there was no time for my call. The operator explained that suicide garnered no urgency. I told them that death in any form required their attention. The operator retorted and told me they'd call me back when there was an open line. That call never came. I called in another hour and the same operator took my call. I tried to find out who was the head of the call department. The operator told me that the department head had committed suicide. He killed his wife first before shooting himself in the head. The operator explained that his wife kept calling and worrying to see when he would be home. He went. She stabbed him then turned the handle of the knife to fuck herself with the broad end. The operator said there was no time for my call, mumbled something about checking the schedule, and promised to call back with a message about the victim. I called back again in an hour and the same operator answered my call. I asked to be connected, pleading that their suicide was within me, and that I am its victim. The operator, flat and cold, replied there was no time for my call. The operator took a message and told me to call back in an hour. But, I was dead. My savior got the message and came to pick me up from my bed.

July 28, 2002
Because You are Evil

"Because you are evil. That's what Papa says. So you are, you're evil, Mom."

I believe my son finds that his father's words are not evil.

But even more I believe that my son's young years do not know what evil is.

Dear Son,

Evil is a manifestation of anger, persecution, and resentment. It exists as a passing spirit of violence, menace and deception. When a person is evil, he wishes for your destruction. His life is fed by the joy derived from your displeasure. Evil is passionate about the death of hope and happiness in your life.

Evil looks forward to your hurt and anger. It devours your purity and encourages you to perpetuate its sinister plan.

Evil derives pleasure from your pain, on a daily basis. It envelops your goodness and reflects it to you with envy.

Evil grows as it is enabled by its own ease of reproduction.

Evil will not do anything for you, but everything against you.

Evil deteriorates your hopes and dreams and then it smiles.

Son, you may not yet understand all of these things, but evil is this.

Evil hopes that you will never realize your dreams.

Evil enjoys that you are hurting inside.

Evil keeps you from being the person you were put here to be.

Now, be mindful that this is what evil really is. I wake up and go to bed with your future in mind. I praise the spirits that allow me to raise you, feed you, teach you, and learn from you. There is not one day that I regret that you are with me. I bow to the altar with you on my mind. I set up my days and nights around you. You bring me joy—from your innocence to your knowledge. I have instilled a joy in you too, and I know they call it "silliness", but it is happiness all the same.

I love you.
Evil does not.

With sincere hopes for your understanding,
Your Mother.

'03

Stop saying that!

Stop telling him that.

You aren't his mom's pimp!

STOP CHANGING
...MY POEMS
...MY ARTICLES
...MY WORDS
...MY WORLD!

2/6/2003
Choking You

Fighting again.

As he came closer to me,
I knew what was coming.
And it did.

The full widened hand
pushing my face backwards,
then the other joining in—
two palms pushing me to the ground.

I roll
but a weighty leg sloppily strides me
and he is sitting on my back
and there goes the wrap.
One, two, sinew hands strangling.

I roll, buckle, and kick.
His knees lock with my head braced there still.
I hang in and fight to stay awake.

He choked harder.
I look up and meeting my gaze
is the little man.
Standing.
Watching.
Crying.
Love all turns to hate.

"Stay, I need…"
A punishing palm covered my shout,

"Here bitch!"
"Take some more shit."
"Yeah bitch!"
"Talk some more shit, now!"

I couldn't breathe. I got a hand free and tried to loosen from his grip.
I shrilled to the universe "Help me!" over and over times ten.

It must have registered somehow because he jumped off.
He darted into the other room.

Night fell.
Re-prize.

In the morning,
my blood was frozen over inside.
Found seepage still wept from a sullen and bloated black eye.
Husband rose his nose in victory.
Stared down at me he came closer before I fully awoke.

Gripped his loneliness firmly to my thigh but there were no churning
waves of joy,
only disdain and paining from the life I'd lost.

Dead on his feet.
Pain hunger now quenched,
he clenched his fists and left the room to find *HIS* son,
still hidden outside with the spirits in the trees.

"I'm alone again!" he roared.

As the wind kicked up,
this wizard pulled his cloak
over his eyes in the breeze.

He sits now,
forever blinded by his brawn and his sickness.

His life and his eyes,
laid to rest for the angels to repurpose.

He has lost his path,
and evil has a firm new place.

The end.

'04

home. Homeless. house.

3/20/2004

Stuck in evolution,

the evolution of being cross and checked like dogs in an auction.

Humans bewildered by the complexity of life.

Growing in the mind yet retracting in intelligence.

Who can challenge you?

I question a new generation of The Man.

Stuck in between the birth of life and death at hand.

Lost chasms of reality not engaged in.

What's the structure we're developing and morphing into?

Who carries your burdens to death?

Whenever Life births, it's meant to be joyous instead.

Now, I'm creeping towards the maker.

Broad entry lights appear while I'm chiding the naysayer.

The savior navigates my fight when the hands wrap tight,

first clenching then hurling to launch my lifeless body into flight.

from one word to that next

I travel by grace

I feel threads pulled through my body

like fibers of change form seams to stitch.

each life, each death, each revolution spun to mend what's within,

to mark my path of deterioration,

to mark my path back to Him one day with a real solution.

3/20/2004

Flight of judgment derails any capture.
Who may enjoy the perfection?
None.

Not without the primary feast,
that last meal,
that last stand,
that feeds the mortal beast.

A lass, stand.

How can a judgment always lead to destruction?

when it
      —aches for chances given, but those given to incorporate none.
      —engages the familiar spirit, that being who travels among us.

My judgment today reeks from the passionate self.
Inside I hide my choice to challenge its accumulated wealth.

Finding new reasons for my long journeys away,
I'm letting poor judgment take an arduous first place.

I thought I chose the right path to stay,
not a lifelong curtsy, bow, and obey.

Not to hide in the frost of weak minds.

No longer in fear of the threat of life's ghost.
Travel with me to the caverns of deep thought.

Shake loose the prejudgments that constantly lead to your rot.

Enjoy the pleasures of your wild, mad lover.

Recognize your worst judgments will only bleed you as the final cost.

124

3/20/2004

Patterns of design
grown to define
a horror house map
inside my mind.

    The ultimate destruction
    is smoke in mirrors
    while the wheels of change
    propel backwards motion.

A decade of feeling
death embroiled my mind
my thoughts enraged
my badge was discouraged.

    How many pain layers
    can be entangled
    when none are listed
    as classified or restricted?

Frustration is driving me
to let go of my being
a reckless mind
inside a wife machine.

    Too poor of confidence
    to know the distinction
    cruelty, indifference,
    or misguided decisions.

If I'm in line,
life feigns new horizons.
But if I'm not,
mirror smoke drifts to violence.

        Forced into alignment
        forced like a penned beast
        force endlessly applied
        I forgive myself the least.

Cannot sway the hurt
cannot mask defeat
getaway is required
all attempts have ceased.

        Love concedes to control
        vows were thin ice sheets
        strangled on the idyllic route
        stranded on unequal footing.

Purpose only rubble
damage nursed by inks
that trace the bold maps buried
within my appropriated body.

        Prey to damaged love
        stifled breaths release
        marriage has defined me
        as indeterminate property.

Cracked dome

Crack, crash, space, gap, gash.

Been scratched, punched and slapped.

Now there's cracked; a breach in my dome.

Green walls we painted in fun, when lives together weren't undone.

I'm slanted, blurred by the fist that spite threw with all its might.

Left and then right, taking turns.

A fight against the tears ruining my cheek's crimson smears.

    "This…!" Slap.

    "That….!" Smack.

Stricken,

my body wants to fold,

to expire.

I topple.

Wall stands tall behind me—bracing my fall.

No bloody street fight here;

it's only you, husband, your brawn.

You! Master yarn caster,

the wizard of nothing at all.

Knock your fists green giant, and

…boom!

Ding…

we're in the ring! Again.

Your knuckles sway and fingers part the air,

furled paws uncover your heinous face sour.

No tape, no bells, no belts that we're after.

It's the whip crack with a strike that's sharp.

The retreat reveals a deeper fissure.

My skull shakes and the blood is streaming,

spoilt my thinking there with an eye socket leaking.

A skin gash flap is finally what breaks up this brawl.

Oh, it' s not over? Bolder, and bolder,

because I won't cower and I won't fight.

Left then right.

I see that beast in you, targeting me,

      You down? Then, stay down! Now do you see?

is his stupidity preparing me for the next strike.

So strong the force,

my consciousness changes course.

He's speaking in muffled sound bites.

He's shouting,

      "You get it nowwwwwWWWW, BITCH!!"

I only get the swelling.

I'm living the pain that will bring new scars by tomorrow morning.

But, why are we fighting?

Have you ever heard the sound of the spirit breaking down?

It's feels like dynamite cracking boulders but there is no sound.

It escapes in the hiss of the wind flattening sails.

Like a full heart of fire expires as it dwindles to kindle.

I know, *you were taunted*, you will claim.

No actor, no script unfolding.

I'm the pile on the ground.

The bruises explain my fear and his loathing.

Pummeling now.

I'm howling.

Broken bones.

Dignity gone.

This me, underneath, it just shatters.

Then his palm hits, an unfurled fist of anger.

My brow cracks, a sound I wish was stranger.

I'm unhinged. Snapped, like an angry parent,

fear quakes me like a lightening crash.

I wake up just enough to escape the next detonate.

My boy creeps down, he stares into my eyes sadly.

His palms stained with my blood as he's grabbing.

"MaaAA!!!!" His shrill......I can't explain it.

I just hang in like I'm under water and he's a searchlight.

He sees the whole wreckage of my life and my few breaths left.

My mask is damaged, it can no longer guard my fears.

"I'm still here," I say, littering the blood and spitting dot print on him.

All the while, I'm still on the ground.

I'm stuck underneath an angry pressed palm wrestling my chin down.

      "Tell her goodbye!" he groans.

My cheek is smashed into my teeth and my face is firmly planted.

His shock, what I see. He's so young.

Rapt. His cries are falling with the shards of my dignity, but they carry me through.

But, he won't forget when pa explodes.

Here It comes again, "move son or this one will be yours!"

He spirals his fist back, a wind-up and then death gores a fist into my side—

no mercy or care.

He laughs as it recoils with my despair.

My brow, dripping and beaten, self-respect piercing.

My mind's eye is pooling violet, even its distracted.

My sides, crack like dominoes, but the violent pro's code is "no broken bones".

All tears I cry are a labyrinth of no exit.

Bones. Breaking blows. Blows breaking hopes.

When pa's white knuckles rear, retreat.

When ma's brow won't cower, it gets beat.

Say, please follow it in to its end to end it, but no, you plan to leave me
here.
Bolts, lightning rage, his explosive haze is deepening the division,
He just says it's me.
I reach to the forehead split and it spills—
a cut, a gap, gash…a fissure.
Snapped.
Really,
a breach of belief against my life,
an Autumn's promise is taken to this violent banter,
    "Get me what I want," and "you better deliver!"
Slanted green eyes, mouth raps shouting, then a SMACK
    "for the burnt toast bitch!"
Slap his fork and he thuds his coffee cup in fervor.
    "Woman!" *smash*
    "Woman?" *thud*
    "WOMAN!!!!" he shrieks.
louder, *crack,*
louder, *crack,*
    "WOMAN!!!!!" he yells,
louder, *crack,*
louder, *crack.*

He's still determined to bury me all-in-one into this sole no identity abyss!
Arching, finally he grabs his own side.
His elbows propped on the chair back and it slams over my stomach.
Caged.
I'm barely making it up from the ground.
Disintegration, but I'm feeling.
I'm feeling.
He leaves. And the bruises change.

I'm vomiting.

I see my son with my dried blood on his hands.

Damn you, my mind's cursed thinking.

"Yeah, my ears are clear, I can hear"

…I think to myself while retreating.

Possessed, now he's creeping nearer to see

if I'll struggle,

if I'll ask for his hand for help to rise.

 "Huh, well I don't hear you now?!" he shouts.

Vexed, he retreats back to his breakfast seat.

 "Well missy," he furls his brow and looks past the table at me on

  the ground.

He glances down at the lump of me and then back down at his breakfast

plate.

I haven't even risen back up from the blood pool,

he's already explaining to me the proper things:

 "What are you supposed to say?" and

 "What are you supposed to do?"

he says, as ignorant of his terror reign,

and our never-ending turmoil.

Gurgling, gurgling, spitting, muttering,

"I am,"

Oh, I better say something because I don't want to hear it. I don't want to feel it…so

come on now!

So I say,

"Yeah. The coffee was cold. I hear you now."

The magnitude of my mind labyrinths for the exit.

It's lightning rage, explosive haze and deepening.

Disintegration of feeling, and

the bruises, and in

being given my proper answers.

June 24, 2004
Calgon

The ripping waves and tides of the ocean are a must in life.

Whether by submersing yourself in the essence of the ocean, getting caught up in the tide,

riding the waves or relaxing in its calms.

The beat of the water and the rush of its intensity—

you can feel all of this from a stare or a swim.

This is a luxury that can only lead to romantic walks

on the beach and being fed tender fruit from the vines,

just as the sun sets, you're heading home now,

you unwind by the fireplace.

The dinner's served complete with fresh jumbo shrimp,

crisp veggies, fine wine and steak.

When it's all said and done, you're massaged and pampered to death,

wrap yourself in the finest silk sheets,

top it off with a thick, soft mink and fall gently to sleep.

'11

homeless. home. struggles.

call your next of kin

7/9/11

Got a black
book for writing.
Je dance, je t'aime. Mon ami, je ne sais pas. Quand le voyage du cinq ans
fini,
voulez-vois, le voir avec moi?
Your power, your words, the connection.

'14

homeless

dust

5/17/2014

I've seen the future and it's looking up.
Caught between the ages, not hardly stuck.
Growing to become sages, now grasping luck.
Stuck between these pages, but not giving up.

To be the best—best stand-in, best woman, the best mom,
I hold my head, wishing to wave a wand and move like a swan.
Hiding in dementia is too scary, so I'll write on,

while the thudding, chugging and huffing
shadow of your former self passes.

If I can free my mind
mend my men
hide inside my skin
perhaps it would help me be the snake charmer that I need within
but that loss of the mind has sensation of sin.

Strangled,
my time is gone.
Discarded,
your evil heart rots here and beyond.

'15

redux

influx

homeless

homeless

homeless

homeless

we moved 30 times

11/2/2015

I grabbed my pen, I held my tongue.
Writing out the times of terror that we'd overcome.

11/22/2015

Shouting down near water, anxious of the ebb and flow.

Shouting about time that springs eternal, quickly changes from null to void.

I wondered how it was or when any man knew the reasons about his visions.

What lengths does he go to keep from chasing these schemes?

It dawned on me once—there in between my bellows.

It hit me hard—twice as hard—

thinking about all of this as I left the wreckage.

That was in no way just a dream.

I took it once…that just didn't matter,

I took it twice…THAT SHOOK ME LOOSE.

I realized things were fractured memories,

Disruption, interruption.

Followed by a high shrill, a gasp, a shatter of the water's surface cracked from the top and suddenly you're sinking heavy beneath.

My heart, you take with you, the rock or cinder block sinking you deeper.

My soul tie twisted, mangled, tangled to your dead-weight.

Now I run my throat dry above the waters ripples.

Screams, cracking and breaking like these waves layering my voice all around you,

covering up your virtue and burying our old dreams at sea.

Maybe I seemed to you, ummm something less…a bitter despair, a fool for love?

Maybe you can think about that now when you rest, at the bottom, making castles in the mud.

I choose to use my memories like a light, to cast hues I can clearly see.

I can visualize the many times I've thought about us, but it fractures to the many times you've deceived me.

My hands pound a clap and my knees skin bare.

Remember me? Begging, pleading, my chest heaving?

When I'm bracing your blows and you're screaming about how you *"just don't fucking care!"*

It's that kind of flow and ebb, where this night cast me down into violence.

A crossed signal, drifting focus, the radio static hums and then fades.

"You won't play me no more" abruptly ends.

Dead and gone. Now you and our undone love are one.

Pushed us right over the edge.

Let the waters fill you with stillness.

My grief and bellows damper easily.

Empty time, empty space, then rigid silence.

Every time I thought I had a hold onto my life,

you used to grip me and choke me.

All hope for me, empty.

That's gone now, I turn as you fade.

My lover, my luck, my faith,

all gone,

gone cold,

and gone away.

Times before I'd trick myself to believe, that leaving you was that last line to cross.

I'd feel you tugging on the heart strings but it was for my purse strings.

You'd snap, break down and become bitter for fear of that loss.

Scorn says,

> *"Don't you dare, I'll take your life! You better think about this man you will cross."*

Every day with you has led to this one,

passing time is the only thing of mine left untouched.

Take a long look and you'll find me sitting at a fountain

or an ocean of wishes, making one last toss.

11/12/15
Null to Void (A Companion Poem). Part 1.

Shouting near the water's edge,
waiting for ebb and flow.
Shouting about time eternal,
transformed from null to void.

Like how it was or when it was,
that anyone knew the reasons about their visions.
Or the perilous extents we will go,
to keep arduous dreams from chasing.

Bobbing in the waves, I yell,
"I took it from you, I took it all!"
The ocean echoes my scream.
I swallow the wet intake.

All of my thoughts are hazards.
Memories, love, and touch are fractured.

I let out a shrill to shatter the water's surface,
but sinking beneath the tow,
I'm willing and hopeless.

My heart, a cinder block, keeps sinking deeper still.
Twisted and mangled,
No beats for the tangled angel.

Yet, a final vision.

Not begging but from thinking.
Chest barrels tubular,
I let loose a crown ring of seaweed.
I remember living and breathing.

But, what is worst?
Bracing your blows or serving the sharks?
Or, listening to you blaring,
about how you just don't fucking care?

Well here I are.
Let the waters fill me with stillness.
Then with me dead and gone,
You and our broken love can rekindle as one.

11/22/2015

I'm here to pluck the daisies,
a garden in my mind, did I grow.
If there's anything like truth that speaks to me,
it ain't your ramble or whine,
it's the dew dripping from those sour grapes,
maybe sweeter if left hanging or ripening on their vines.

Nighttime hold me steady,
hop on my midnight ride.
Trapped in the vortex of that eddy,
heal my hands, hold up the light.
Raindrops left from the brutal burst,
plick and patter as they hit the ground without course.
Its deafening song strikes my chord,
but heals the horrors with its drip devotions
for burnt out fear and scattering emotions.

Call me up, part me out, shore my shameful wool.
Wrap me up, take me hollow, toss me out for good.
I have no more ties to angels, just viper in my blood.

Unanswered prayers are naked memories
of
seraphim
singing,
blocking gates to serenity,
dissolving prayers to infinity,
dispelling ones made curiously,
of believing that I'm no good.
But, that's not true, I can still rise with more tethers secured.

I'm strewn but too listless to stray.

Too long gone to obey.

Sunlight it dawns and twilight falls short with a weathered report.

The deep earth it hides me but no plots filled with food.

Keep the daisy in your hair, salute my slab if you prefer,

just leave me here in an ocean of good.

11/22/15

When are you going to take up my cause?

Why are you without an epic demonstration?

Why do I only get your forked tongue flicking words into my timid ear

to sway me to say only what you want to hear?

What do you miss most about me?

Aren't I just a hole of easy retreat?

When are you going to finish this terror?

Why take pause and declare your innocence?

Don't you care what happens when this hot venom rages deep

in your mind? in your veins?

It carries you to this ailing slavery by way of my cold-hearted killing,

body trampled over by your inhumanity.

You're already dead to the world,

embezzling my dignity,

destroying all reason,

the demands of the pulsing muscle,

the unnamed demon.

When are you going to rid yourself of this beast?

Never?

Don't doubt, resign right now!

Found are they now,

too strong to ignore,

cut the throat of grace,

it takes revenge by way of your grimace.

It's a new form of waste.

Oh dignity, oh dignity, where do you scatter?
Are you searching for a blessing from the priest?
Taking me lifeless beyond the tall grass.

It is life that bends and crushes me beneath your weight?
Out of sight…right?
No one will hear me.
I almost missed my mind for a moment when it'd tell the eyes to shut off
to this scornful hate.
Relent to the empty you,
but you're new and renewed from angst.
Wrenching the last of my life towards mortality.
"Are you in there still?"
You'll ask my soulless being.
Will you hold together now only laced from the lies that you once told
me?

More wringing.
More banging.
Leftovers,
traces from the pattern of boudoir lace that covered up the loss of my
innocence.
Red lips would be smeared from his unfaithful kiss.
If I say no, will you horror or glory in those words?
You turn more brutal than blades beneath my feet.
Hold onto the ode, the odious,
the clay earth's cremation,
those underground mysteries that you slither towards for greater
recognition.

Long before any death bell,

its grip had you hooked.
It's draining, but this pain is much lesser than this life,
the one stolen from me
at first look.

Weep now. Weep never.

I weep gently passing the pain of you,
delivered from this acrimony,
forgotten is our matrimony.

Place your immaturity on the guillotine,
lob it away with the rites of a spring fling.
I'm sharing my volition as a point of contention.
Not to be taken lightly like a papal vision.

Who must we embrace when the times around us fail?
Why must we only find reason at the tolling bell.

'15

hotel

last night someone knocked and threatened to call the cops

he's acting out.
No. No, I won't do it!!

all of him jumps on us

--

Help her!

Fuck her!

Help her!

Fuck her!

Help her!

--

I'm awake!

Wet hair on a frayed towel.

I finally call for help while he slept.

--

"Hey, it's been a while. Can I please come and see you

right now?"

11/30/15 (order?)

Designate that stone core pillow for someone willing,
it's still propped up my heavy head.

Holding on, letting go,
it's just real trauma that is for sure.

Taking leave, taking heed,
then regret died as an expressive confession to the love I have for myself.

Holding on, letting go,
just real trauma that is for sure.

Taking leave,
goodbye possession greed,
the time is now to let me go.

11/30/15

Today, sadness reached me, the first time since I ran away from you screaming.

Seeing my life and you tearing pages away, those images of you are still there.

Though these tears scorch across face, redden eyes, and force me to face,

I see what's being forgotten on the inside, of what once was alive, now rotten.

I need to beware.

A slow drag brings back my focus.

This is not a joke.

Memories enter giving me an injection of reflection.

The fight so many times fought.

The tears replace what was bitter and broken—

the lost, bought, sold and distraught.

To *the boss, the Master,* I once had

I'm free today from your grasp.

Well, he may never know or care what the world says about my proclamation's legitimacy.

Guess what, I'm free! I'll declare it for me:

Unto myself I deserve,

to live alive, not dead.

Emotions on hold, barren but still bold, just held in reserve.

I may never again greet or wish to visit this tiring emotional retreat.

These are my tears staining my cheeks in streaks,

I flitter them away,

they fall like glitter from my briskness.

I can get carried away. There's a scent of dangerous infection.

It's arrived here, undoubtedly a remission—
our union lost, solidarity withered to dissention.

I've been fierce. I've been strong.
I'm taking care of the drawn-out return to self,
this barren and desolate acre.
Rocks crumble beneath me as reception,
the tiger inside prepares to ambush any gaze lasting too long in my
direction.
Transmute into a 'no-more-love beast' if I must.

You there…who cast hate, shame or doubt will be mired in mirrored
dejections.
I won't hurt long from you.
I will repair what's broken too.

As long as I live and even past deaths' beyond,
I am the tiger to guide my own intentions.
What say you to me now? That same bitter growl?
I can't hear you. I'm cage free now, so you fetch.
I am forlorn in my quest,
but realizing myself rising as the hunter,
not prey, no toy for catch.

Is it my arrival or my sudden leave that bothers?

It's that luck I carried with me.
I suppose it forgot to take your side on this, so take it in stride.
Do you…*blah, blah, blah*…about almighty powers?
Mine is stronger.
Mine. I suggest you direct your customs to your own people.

I carry on strong. I know where I belong.

From behind these tears, behind these hidden fears,

to remember the trick was before the church steeple.

It was real before this.

Long ago, far away, so long,

gone.

11/30/15

Cold, tired,
shades drawn.
My cold sweat beads down through the blades of grass on the freshly
mowed lawn.
Thinking.
Clothes gone,
bed empty in there,
and shades drawn.
Still?
I'm feeling sickly.
Been drinking venom from a tin cup crimped at the edges
from being busted over the head of a drunk at the bar.
I'm looking everywhere for his shadow, in fear.
That anchor weight is still heavy.

11/30/15

Sometimes simple is enough.
The bastard draws, I press my luck.
If I said fewer words we'd be through,
not called out to be picturing my doom.

Last time I got in this paranoid mess, I pulled a priest aside to confess.
A shame how things change.
That one moment, realizing when the new game's on, but it ain't named.
No options but guilt as I steady for my quick demise.
I have a split second to wrap my head around the bleak situation
that's got a pistol drawn.

This is no joke, luck found me broke,
quick wits ain't enough to avoid this deadly surprise.

Simple, I thought to myself. If simple, I'd have already left.
Simple thoughts, simple dreams, but no more time.

As simple as it gets, this fear fills the well in my chest.
Taking my life will be my last thought tonight or just my best regret.

Come back around when my memory fades.
Come back around to seek doomsday's trade.

It's been my life for his up to now,
this is my chance to not miss,
but it's my life going forward, without ending.
Not this ending. Not this.

11/30/2015

I heard six sneaky, tick-tocks past the mark.
I'm heading down southbound scorching tire tracks.
I heard a gun cock and unload.
I'm gone.
I saw visions of the spatter, bones shatter and my mind explode.
Like a grainy motorcade.

Nothing left for me
but the wind at my back.
Chasing the demons I can't escape
and the reality I lack.
My own black cherry, firm and sweet,
turned out to have a stone,
plucked by some fellow too early, then raped,
and repeated as revenge when I'm barely over 10,
an innocence you may have sought can't be brought back.

The visions feel real, I'm totally consumed.
Yet, bloody hands continue reaching
until I'm the one below a head stone.

Make your lies silent now.
Make your cries so too.
I'm making new memories, alone, without you.

11/30/15

I've been brought out of the cages.

Visitors? Sages? Anyone awaiting my return to the temple of truth?

I tear myself from their chatter and take up the actions I had long ago

scattered.

Before wandering wanton and wasted during my youth,

so many lost yesterday's away.

I don't need any cunning donation.

My fighting ways don't require you nor any misdirected intentions.

I empower over my own.

I will leave you alone.

I will commit to this change by channeling love and strength back to my

existence.

Are you so powerless in your infinity that you have to pass along your

calamities to me?

Was your ill intent an accident?

Or meant throughout the years for me to feel, but for no one else to see?

Do you need this being of mine in order to be mature before the hands

of time?

Does it give you an ill license of some kind?

Are you daydreaming through the possibility that is already extinct?

Does this paradise have an expiration?

You demanded some sort of proclamation.

Don't you find yourself already armed with the answers?

All were well spoken and succinct before.

I have to be myself and go.

Empowered, full and righteous, and protected.

Every one of this free women's step is self-liberation.

What you produce without me doesn't cross my mind.

You never cared for a moment in our past, so I'm done.

Two decades in a temple of terror. Now, I'm free.

I'm ready to embrace myself and others who pull me in close,

to see their strange face when they gaze longingly,

saying *"it's been too damn long since you've come home."*

Home? Yes, at home within myself.

Some say I am at this crossroads, a fork in the path.

Beaten down, they still see,

but in plenty of time

they'll help repair my broken doses of reality.

I found a song inside which needs to be heard, it needs to be.

I'm empowered by the harmony of sweet reprieve.

It strengthens my heart with just enough ferocity to break away.

It's not the easiest thing to do when overthinking keeps me tethered,

but it's not a noose.

I've dreamt many years of a homecoming to my former self.

Here it is…like a monk finding their damaged temple still standing.

In peace now. I've survived the archival.

Though overwhelmed with this life's fruits,

Hope opens its arms and welcomes me back like a tired, former recruit.

Down in one count and I was just debris.

Now, I take the melody of living to my soul,

I feel it searching the length of my spine,

trickling down through every crevice of my back,

through to my heart and body.

I let the impact on my eyes set to reflect.

I shudder to think that I haven't let myself feel this deep.

What remains for me now?

My personal thunder, my found voice

lift me up with the Congo beat to dancing feet,

by the powers of my mind I can finally rest and retreat.

It's a better use of my time when I follow music down the fine line,

heart open for mending

not battered, shattered, and banging.

To languish in laughter, yet constant fear creeps back up on me.

I know more than anything,

it's the prose of my bitterness that shouts out loudly.

My hands remain ready, red from wringing and wiping the liquid pain

away from my face.

"Mirror, you can believe it's me," I sing, *"it's me again!"*

Now, I'm going to conqueror and take fate firmly in my own hands.

I want to treat it with the respect it deserves,

to remove the limits that I once had no way around.

Yes, I skirted with haste, the tiger bowed, and finally the monk smiled.

Power is within me now.

Fix the latch on the union gate because it's not locked anymore, it just

shakes.

Opened up enough barred doors for me to escape.

If I feel the urge to creep back out,

here and there to breathe in a quick reprieve,

I mean, if I ever feel this low,

I'll remember the depths of my soul where I glow,

and return to my true ways, so clear and imminent now.

Let me crawl from under this old camouflaged skin—it's useless and

abused.

I'm so charred from it that I had to change the name of the game.

I've returned to myself and the ways I was raised.

Alone,

where a dancing spirit rises to wrestle the distorted me to its grave.

Some want to help,

others want to own my hurt.
But, it's no matter to you,
it's mine to heal and protect.
And in the end, the Spirit called my name,
I'm back to rise again.
Oh yes, I am. alone. at home within. here I am.

12/1/15

There's just a shell of me now.

Don't come to me thinking,

I've got to let you waltz through the door.

Show yourself out the way you turned your back on me,

shrinking.

Tell all those lies to another boar.

I realize now, it's you,

glad to hang me out when I didn't do more.

Trying to find a reason to believe that you can be anything but a plea outside the entry.

Walk back out the way you came in,

they'll bury me in the ground before I bend another knee.

Begging you? I won't waste a second, I'm taking this all like a kid in a candy store.

What a mightier web of lies you weave when there's a goodbye from me.

Get your hand out of my wallet and show yourself, then be sure to quietly go.

Are you begging, pleading or otherwise in need of some affection?

Am I supposed to easily loosen my grip on the double barrel I'm to keep disposed?

Take your long legs,

your lying eyes, your jagged edge,

and your pity cries,

back to the man who was once "<u>you</u>" so long before!

12/1/2015

It's a creole girl that's blown my world,
my arms wound tight around her waist.
Those tiger eyes lock,
the fever pitch,
then she cries.
But I am lust, I kill love.
And, I need a taste for proof.
I think the day has come,
better now than none
when I take her back to my room.

12/1/2015

It was dawn when the bayou blushed.
The sweeping broom beat down the carpet's dust.

12/1/2015

My Words

166

You can't! Make a true believer out of the cynical me.
You can't! Take my wisdom and good sense away.
You can't! Hold me hostage when I say I don't love you.
I can't! Be the one your dreams have created of me.
I can't! Be the true love no more I am the wrecking crew.
I can't! Show you faith that I'll never again put into you.
I won't! Convince you to stay when I don't want it.
I can! Be the one to move on and show you out.
I won't! Be the one left with a thing to prove.

12/1/2015

Tragedy strikes
held in a tight place
pillow on my face
rigid under the weight
stifle my vocals
end your doubts
dead on you now
I'll be at God's gates

12/1/2015

Did they find you weeping beneath the trees before the storm?

Are you the still child of the dawn?

What happened when the young came to call?

Did he take you down fighting? Did he take it all?

Can't you speak any about it now or are the words and thoughts too clouded?

What will become when the truth shows itself to all around?

Is this the time I take the law into my hands?

Is this the time to turn the hour glass of sand?

You say *innocence lost; that's it, nobody cares.*

So what's left? Maybe I'll take the matter up, 'cuz it's past time.

When I find that lowly bastard,

I'll have his head for justice, for my baby and for myself.

12/1/15

Took away the lonely tree planted on my front lawn.
Take my life away from inside the circle of lies that confine me.
Draw a knife to my throat when he thinks I'd cheat.
Fires lead into the night when he thinks another's seen smiling.
Keep your dumb jealousy in check, you know I work till dawn.

12/1/15

Good words broken, vows shard like mirrors.
Broke truths and lies scattered wide,
my truth pierced his armor.

Can you forget me now? Are emotions running wild?
Do you relent from me as a useless parody?
Is there a shred of honor in your talk?
An ounce of righteousness in your heart?
Time to regress like the last drop of wine in your glass?
Kept me wanting, waiting and defending that broken image of our past.
I left a shadow of doubt and reason crashed.
I left a shadow of reason and doubt eased my fall.
I felt a quiver of warmth when I dialed out that call.
It tears me down to know you believe that you're the bigger one and I'm
the small.

I can't stop thinking about this ego mess.
Pain gently bleeds from my heart,
doesn't need to hit the air before this frame rusts.

Getting off this ride fast,
I'm wreckage from the hurricane.
I will remember these nights throughout time,
you shaking my grace and sanity,
no logic left behind.

Why did I come here tonight?

I used to confess the aches and quakes of love
to carry us through the day and night, noon to dusk.

Until your obsession with my possession thrust us to dust.

Your greedy ego tried to capture my spirit fleeting,
but I will never forget your hands on my throat,
shaking loose my sanity.

I will remember the best,
that I have finally escaped.
Barren and empty,
yet I know I've taken flight.

Though your memory lingers.
I've said my peace,
I let it go.
Know,
this is the final tonight.

INTERLUDE

Carry the torch of remorse and act like it never occurred?
Can't take back the stupid things that I said.
Now I'm here left with the dance of the pen,
taunting me to be a woman of my word.
Carry the torch of remorse and act like it never occurred?
Can't take back the stupid things that I said.

12/2/15
Quill Dance (A Companion Poem) Take 1.

Slowly dancing towards the paper, descends the pen.
Truth draws it nearer.
Timid is my hand, it assumes control but my eyes just stare.

Lines are drawn, ink is clear.
I have no power left to shut out the words I hear.
Letters describe emotions I can't bear.

My lungs fill with a long-drawn breath, now, for courage.

My shaky hand confronts the pen.

Words,
close the hole in my heart where love had been,
remove aches I dare not escape and fights I can't win,
release me from the armor I'm captive within.

Or,
take the knife from my back,
and use its bloody tip,
but let these brutal thoughts spill.

The eruption I begged for finally takes place.
Hearing my thoughts race,
but the pen can't keep pace!
Burying my head and waiting for the worst,
that I'll lose them all along with my voice.

Cured,

It's taunting me to be a woman of my word.

It flows and strokes,

uncovers expressions so potent,

in synch every moment,

and together refined,

we lit a torch to remorse.

12/2/15

Are you going to forget me someday?
I hope you will, starting today.
Won't you go on and let me forget you?
I'm so ready to leave here and leave *you t*o you.
Take what you can and never see my face again,
the smile that you defiled.
Are you going to forget me someday?
I hope you will, so I will it in this way.

'16

1/16/2016

In the dream
In the dream
She started talking, giving much lip to her mind's tragedy stalking her towards death.
In the dream
In the dream
She kept on walking, fighting relentlessly against fear but suicide stayed right where she had left it.
This is the story
This is the story in which
She was sure that depression was temporary, that she'd escape back to happiness where everything else was the same.
This is the story
This is the story in which
She cut her life short without a voice,
not a tale of a failing career, old age or ailing health to blame.

This is the gun
This is the gun with
This is the gun with which she took her own life
This is the gun
This is the gun with
This is the gun with which she got better odds on death than she did as a wife.
For her quest to die, without shame, on her own terms,
Not at behest, as her best quest, no last requests.

This is where
This is where I am still
This is where I am still living without living,

just seething, no joy or warmth purposely careening.
Before this I was able to keep laughing despite his torture.
So I'm restless.
This is
This is how I'm due
This is how I'm due to die with those decades old memories, that petrified
look given to me,
if found in a cold pool of crimson,
the gunshot's void,
own self the victim.

This is
This is just
This is just what's left of his mom.

March 22, 2016

Black and Blues (Three Ways)

(To the ex)

I've got the blues today,
and the torrential rain of teardrops fall
Black and blue,
I am, bruised—"But hey",
he says, "it's only because you refused my calls!"

Taken down, I'm tasting bitter ends.
I should know better,
I should know to never think thoughts again.
And never my own.

I kept the promises marriage made
and whenever asked, I delivered.
But I'm dying under your fist,
my spirit is strong,
but this is the end, nearer.

I take the stings and pick myself up,
then I fall and time crawls.
And you let me know with pummels,
whenever my progress stalls.

I'm low down, pride beaten,
never low enough for you.
The cracking bones beneath skin is the usual,
love is never enough proof.

I'm dizzy, he hates me.
I'm crawling to the door.
I hear his shoes,
dragging behind me,
dragging over the ground.

Fading now.
No, I don't turn around.
A crack in my crown,
knowing I am at the smallest pore between never and now.

In the crimson spatter,
I just cannot set myself free or see somehow.
An empty shell to be,
I'm black and blue.
Misery bends to me and whispers,
"you're unworthy."

No.
I won't apologize while you rationalize your wins.
I'm going strong again no matter the prediction or the changing direction
of the winds.

I won't apologize while you're rationalize about just how strong your will
is over our vows.
I'm taking my dignity pieces. I'm cashing out this sacrificing right now.

I can't predict where my fragments will fall,
Or, how long I can endure your fist and its face-pounding sickness.

I won't apologize while you rationalize on any day.
I hope I wake up one morning and get away,
because all that's left here, to be realistic,
is just to become a toe-tagged statistic.

4.23.2016
An End

Demand of death,
an end to the clamor.
You say I'm disassembled,
I don't resemble your perfect wife.
While shuttered in this hell, with its hounds sent for tearing and gnawing,
my meat to marrow for their nourish,
their only meal is my life.

On a spit you'll roll and roast one day.
Here's a toast to incite the God's to anger.

This is just a moment of distinction to you.
The one where I tell you to stop being cruel,
but you squeeze harder for an end
and demand death for my dying glamor.

Begging,
my face greets a coffee stain on the ground where you spun around,
because your cup was empty and I didn't refill it quickly enough!
Grabbing,
you exclaim you will "take my life without a sound!"
So much for the sail wind's creeping through this veil, it's undone, so turn
me loose!
It was a long ago dream in my mind,
like a roadside car crash.
I saw the us justly demised to a single crowd face.
I left one leg dangling off the edge of an overpass to nowhere,
thinking of the options and swinging the other over to meet two feet.

"Say no more," was on my mind but like dream ruse
instead you leapt,
with some driver yelling "it's time" while you fell.
The red light blew, blue light read, time stood still,
but instead I was forced to choose.
"Is there a future for you two?" asked the Suit.
I knew you'd had your day, but,
I also know the break and cracks of vertebrate.

Had it been me and not a dream that night,
with any options up, I would not be in sight.

Instead I live on bended knee and hearing cries,
now you want me to tell the Suit to leave the noose
to sway without its taste of your abuse? I have no love left.
Maybe I lost it to the milk and cream when I was stirring,
teetering left and right constantly serving you.
If I slip a drop your anger waves crash,
with intent to drown me without sound escaping.
Instead, it's
          "How dare you serve me this bitter venom shit,"
well my choices were made since you demanded to make them!

Awake,
I see your body,
it can roast in red,
singe flesh to your rest,
now it's your cries no longer heard.
Your dust will settle,
ashes dome the size of a pen tip,
dancing demon dogs will have eaten,

no scraps for reheating,

your empty void heart,

taken away and recycled,

for some new child to return to the wild,

without the terror I found,

without the terror you made,

and all the terror from which I ran away.

Wrestling with you days to years and years-to-date.

Enough!

I fall to the floor, but no damage.

I'm only wretched from the sight of you bearing down on me.

I'm looking to a heaven beyond your senses.

I was hoping that once you were done,

down here in the coffee stain writhing,

You would just simply let me go and forget us.

4/24/2016

…I listen closely.

I know he is gone.

There will be signs,

there will be tones,

but it is surely too late.

There may never be a sound from his great unknown.

I return. The angels relay.

It's a matter of time if ever someone finds his true physical state.

Recognition unknown.

I have heard the last word.

The battling seagulls shrill,

maybe laughing instead.

Like a baby reborn,

and my fate retold,

I declared my journey would end,

Alive.

It was not my own life.

But, it's too late to be won.

I hear nothing else in mind except

this vicious time is over and done.

'17

8/20/2017

Sometimes when you stop to smell the roses
you only come face-to-face
with the gnarl of the beast that roam there.

September 2017
Black Book Poetry Break

Blues smile and
tears wall the flowers.
Sand silken knees drag the sheets
with a visionary sublime crawl.
The peddler's care
was a prayer for parasites
compared to him.
A Venus uncaged explodes to a fire fox
when the hammer drops
like a melody, a harmony.

I'm frozen, when decreed at last,
all stolen security is unleashed.
Released in every degree from the Master,
a no man, a *one-two* man, so no one else could woo man
with no doubt that my fears would shield my glow.
Hung joy for death but the curse spread.

You need to know.

Never will I endure,
time cannot repair this damage,
especially now with the past set to rest.

May 2017
Roadkill

Don't play with me.
I'll gore that socket
and puncture that intact pocket.
I'll leak the deceit that is you
and let it ooze.

The cornea will split.
Blood pool in the top and bottom lids.

You will lumber away
chest caved
and dead.

A thud ends your fall.

I'll be crisscrossing you in victory,
Roadkill,
Not stalled!

They'll be figuring time of death
by the scavengers buzzing overhead,
by the volume of carcass left,
by the hover of flies and,
the flitter of gnats,
g o r g i n g,
after an initial attack,
engrossed in an obsession of sensations.

Creatures close in
to ponder your stench,
to follow red streaks,
to your rotting flesh meat.

Beaks stabbing,
wings flapping,
battles happening,
while steady devouring
what is left of your defeat.

Now Hear Me!
I will stand assured and not come undone.

There will be no more utterances from a bruised battered woman.

www.ingramcontent.com/pod-product-compliance
Lightning Source LLC
Chambersburg PA
CBHW070629310726
48982CB00001B/222